THE EARLIEST
GREGORY THE

In his role of apostle of the English and promoter of Augustine's mission, Pope Gregory the Great became the subject of what is one of the earliest pieces of literature surviving from the Anglo-Saxon period: a *Life* written by an unknown author of Whitby around 680–704. Although crude in its Latinity and idiosyncratic in its presentation, this work is a fascinating source of early traditions about the conversion of the English – including the famous story of Gregory's encounter with the Anglian slave boys – and an important witness to the veneration felt for the saint himself. It casts valuable light on English history in the seventh century, particularly on the career of Edwin of Northumbria, and it is the source of two of the most famous legends of the Middle Ages, the Mass of St Gregory and the story of Trajan's rescue from hell. The *Life* of Gregory seems to be the earliest of the Saints' lives of this period and it is in many ways the most remarkable.

THE EARLIEST LIFE OF GREGORY THE GREAT

By an Anonymous Monk of Whitby

TEXT, TRANSLATION AND NOTES BY
BERTRAM COLGRAVE
formerly Reader in English, University of Durham

CAMBRIDGE UNIVERSITY PRESS

CAMBRIDGE

LONDON   NEW YORK   NEW ROCHELLE
MELBOURNE   SYDNEY

CAMBRIDGE UNIVERSITY PRESS
Cambridge, New York, Melbourne, Madrid, Cape Town, Singapore, São Paulo

Cambridge University Press
The Edinburgh Building, Cambridge CB2 8RU, UK

Published in the United States of America by Cambridge University Press, New York

www.cambridge.org
Information on this title: www.cambridge.org/9780521309240

© University of Kansas Press 1968

This publication is in copyright. Subject to statutory exception
and to the provisions of relevant collective licensing agreements,
no reproduction of any part may take place without the written
permission of Cambridge University Press.

First published by The University of Kansas Press 1968
First paperback edition published by Cambridge University Press 1985
Re-issued in this digitally printed version 2007

A catalogue record for this publication is available from the British Library

Library of Congress Catalogue Card Number: 67–24360

ISBN 978-0-521-30924-0 hardback
ISBN 978-0-521-31384-1 paperback

Preface

IT SEEMS REMARKABLE that no critical, annotated edition of the earliest Life of Gregory the Great has so far appeared, seeing that it has been eighty years since the attention of scholars was drawn to its importance. Besides having some claim to be the earliest extant piece of written literature produced by the Anglo-Saxons, it is also the source of two of the most famous legends of the Middle Ages, the Mass of St. Gregory and the story of Trajan's rescue from hell. It throws a few gleams of welcome light on church life in Northumbria in the seventh and early eighth centuries and, though the writer is no Bede, yet in his own simple way he reflects the attitude of his time to two outstanding figures, Gregory the Great and King Edwin, and the honour in which they were held by his own countrymen. His biography reflects too the difficulties that faced an early writer who attempted to build up a written literature to replace the native oral tradition and adapt it to the use of the recent converts to Christianity.

The fact that there is only one manuscript of the *Life* only adds to the difficulties of the editor, and the production of a text which is more or less intelligible has not been easy. It has been possible to make a few emendations based mostly upon the frequent scriptural quotations and upon the author's tendency to quote passages from Gregory's work and to echo his phrases. The earliest users of the *Life*—Paul the Deacon's Interpolator and John the Deacon—were often uncertain as to the writer's meaning. But, on the whole, the narrative sections of the *Life* are compara-

tively straightforward, and the worst obscurities are mostly confined to the writer's theological and philosophical comments.

The text is based on a collation of the original MS at St. Gall. I am very grateful to the authorities of the Stiftsbibliothek for putting every facility at my disposal; I am also grateful to Sir Roger Mynors for allowing me to make use of his collation of the text made some years ago. The original has no chapter divisions, but, for the sake of convenience and ease in reference, I have used those made by Ewald and followed by Gasquet, even though they leave something to be desired. In one instance only have I altered Gasquet's arrangement, where he attaches the first sentence of c. 22 by mistake to the end of c. 21.

My thanks are due to Paul Meyvaert for various suggestions and to Sister Hildegarde W. Parry, O.S.B., of St. Cecilia's Abbey, Ryde, Isle of Wight, who has given me much valuable help and advice, especially in matters dealing with the author's Latin style and liturgical borrowings. I would also like to thank Professor Bruce Dickins and Professor Dorothy Whitelock for reading through my manuscript and making valuable suggestions and particularly the latter for calling my attention to the insertion in the Cambridge MS (Kk 4, 6) which helped to clear up the enigmatic and otherwise unintelligible references to St. Jerome in c. 28.

I am also grateful for the willing help given me by the staff of the Cambridge University Library. I am indebted to the London Library for the long-term loan of basic books and works of reference—the provision of a unique service which during more than a century a multitude of scholars have had reason to appreciate. It would

indeed be a tragedy if, owing to lack of funds, this service had to be discontinued.

In undertaking the publication of this book, the University of Kansas Press has preserved my happy association with the University, extending over several years. I am grateful to the staff for their careful work and particularly to Professor Clyde Hyder for the immense pains he has taken in preparing my copy for the press and for his many very helpful suggestions.

BERTRAM COLGRAVE

Cambridge, England

Abbreviations

ASC	Whitelock, D., ed. (with D. C. Douglas and S. I. Tucker), *The Anglo-Saxon Chronicle* (London, 1961).
Bede Opp.	Giles, J. A., ed., *Venerabilis Bedae opera quae super sunt*, 12 vols. (London, 1843-44).
BHL	*Bibliotheca Hagiographica Latina*, ed. Socii Bollandiani, vols. 1, 2 and supp. (Brussels, 1898-1911).
BLTW	*Bede, his Life, Times and Writings*, ed. A. Hamilton Thompson (Oxford, 1935).
Brechter	Brechter, S., *Die Quellen zur Angelsachsenmission Gregors des Grossen* (Beiträge zur Geschichte des alten Mönchtums und des Benediktinerordens, Münster, 1941).
Bright	Bright, W., *Chapters of Early English Church History*, 3rd ed. (Oxford, 1897).
Cabrol	Cabrol, F., et Leclercq, H., *Dictionnaire d'Archeologie chrétienne et de Liturgie*, 15 vols. (Paris, 1907-53).
DCB	Smith, W., and Wace, H., *Dictionary of Christian Biography*, 4 vols. (London, 1877-87).
Eddius	Colgrave, B., ed., *The Life of Bishop Wilfrid by Eddius Stephanus* (Cambridge, 1927).
EHD I	Whitelock, D., *English Historical Documents I, c. 500-1042* (London, 1955).
ERE	Hastings, J., ed., *Encyclopaedia of Religion and Ethics*, 13 vols. (Edinburgh, 1908-26).
Ewald	Ewald, P., "Die älteste Biographie Gregors I," *Historische Aufsätze dem Andenken an Georg Waitz gewidmet* (Hannover, 1886), pp. 17-54.
Gasquet	Gasquet, F. A., ed., *A Life of Pope St. Gregory the Great* (Westminster, 1904).
HAA	*Historia abbatum auctore anonymo*. See under Plummer.
HAB	*Historia abbatum auctore Beda*. See under Plummer.

HE	*Historia ecclesiastica gentis Anglorum auctore Beda.* See under Plummer.
Liber Pontificalis	Mommsen, T., ed., *MGH. Gestorum Pontificum Romanorum I* (Berlin, 1898).
MGH	*Monumenta Germaniae historica.* Auct. Ant. Auctores antiquissimi. Epp. Epistolae. Poet. Lat. Poetae Latinae. SRM. Scriptores rerum Merovingicarum.
PG	*Patrologia graeca,* ed. Migne, J. P., 161 vols. (Paris, 1857-86).
PL	*Patrologia latina,* ed. Migne, J. P., 221 vols. (Paris, 1844-64).
Plummer	Plummer, C., ed., *Baedae Historia Ecclesiastica gentis Anglorum: Venerabilis Baedae opera historica,* 2 vols. (Oxford, 1896).
RS	*Chronicles and Memorials of Great Britain and Ireland during the Middle Ages* (Rolls Series) (London, 1858-96).
Stenton	Stenton, F. M., *Anglo-Saxon England* (Oxford, 1947).
Tangl	Tangl, M., ed., *S. Bonifatii et Lulli Epistolae, MGH Epp. selectae, I* (Berlin, 1916).
Taylor	Taylor, H. M., and J., *Anglo-Saxon Architecture,* 2 vols. (Cambridge, 1965).
Two Lives	Colgrave, B., ed., *Two Lives of St. Cuthbert* (Cambridge, 1940).
VA	*Vita sancti Cuthberti auctore anonymo.* See *Two Lives.*
VP	*Vita sancti Cuthberti prosaica auctore Beda.* See *Two Lives.*

Contents

Preface	v
Abbreviations	viii
Introduction	
I HISTORICAL BACKGROUND	1
II GREGORY THE GREAT	19
III WHITBY	31
IV AUTHOR AND DATE	45
V SOURCES	50
VI THE AUTHOR'S LATIN STYLE	55
VII THE RELATION BETWEEN BEDE AND THE WHITBY WRITER	56
VIII LATER HISTORY OF THE LIFE	59
IX THE MANUSCRIPT	63
Latin text	72
Translation	73
Notes	140
Select Bibliography	166
Appendix	168
Index	173

INTRODUCTION

I. HISTORICAL BACKGROUND

THE STORY of the meeting of Gregory the Great with the young English lads in the Roman marketplace and his famous series of puns forms a picturesque if legendary beginning to a train of events that was to alter the whole face of Europe. Gregory may well have had in his mind the vague outline of a plan which could, if it succeeded, save both Rome and civilized Europe as he knew it. He saw the mighty world empire of Rome tottering to its fall, but instead of sitting by and waiting for the end, he conceived the idea of winning the young and vigorous nations for Christ and establishing a new Roman Empire, this time an empire based on the rock foundation of Christ and the Church. He saw Rome ruling a spiritual kingdom won, not by the sword but the tireless efforts of missionaries making dangerous and arduous journeys to the uttermost parts of the known world and risking their lives among heathen peoples. He was only too ready to accept such risks himself. The story of his vain attempt to go in person to the English people (c. 10) may not be historical but is certainly true to character.

Those fair-haired youths whom he saw in Rome were subjects of Ælle, King of Deira, one of the two kingdoms of which the Anglian province of Northumbria originally consisted;[1] it covered roughly the area of modern Yorkshire, while the kingdom of Bernicia extended to the north, though its exact limits are not certain. Bernicia was

---

[1] P. Hunter Blair, *Anglo-Saxon England*, pp. 42 ff.

ruled over by King Ida. When Æthelfrith, his grandson, came to the throne of Deira in 593, he united the two kingdoms by marrying Ælle's daughter Acha; also, by bloody fighting, he established the supremacy of the English invaders over the Celtic peoples whom they had supplanted. The Anglian conquerors were, as Gregory knew, heathen, but he was probably not aware that the British races whom they and the other Germanic invaders conquered were Christian. The Christianity which had flourished in Britain up to the middle of the fifth century lost touch with Rome and the Gaulish Church when the Anglo-Saxon invasions largely cut the British Christians off from the Continent, thus making it very difficult for them to acquire any but the vaguest knowledge of what was going on in Europe. It is not surprising, therefore, that the Celtic Church, though not differing in any essentials from the orthodox beliefs of the Catholic Church, had none the less developed certain differences in practice, such as the shape of the tonsure, the formula used in baptism, and particularly the use of a different table or cycle for fixing the date of Easter. Nor did the Celtic Church accept the supremacy of the Bishop of Rome as the ruler of the Western Church.[2]

It is not surprising that Gregory should have had little knowledge about conditions in Britain. Some information, probably not always accurate, may have reached Rome through the association of the Frankish royal house with the kingdom of Kent. And it is possible that stories, perhaps highly exaggerated, were carried by British and Irish pilgrims to such places as the monastery at Lérins.[3] But it

---
[2] Plummer, II, 348 ff.
[3] Bright, p. 47.

Historical Background

is quite clear that, when Gregory sent his band of missionaries under the leadership of Augustine in 597, such information as they had was not calculated to encourage them. They had not gone far before their courage failed them altogether. Bede tells us how they were paralyzed with terror at the thought of going to a barbarous, fierce, and unbelieving nation whose language they did not even know. So they sent Augustine back to ask Gregory to relieve them of this dangerous mission. But Gregory sent them a firm but encouraging reply urging them not to allow themselves to be frightened by the difficulties of the journey and by any horror stories about the land to which they had to go.[4]

When, after a long and perilous journey, the party landed in Britain, they found a highly civilized court in Kent ruled over by King Æthelberht, who was in close touch with the Christian religion, though he was not himself a Christian. His wife Bertha, daughter of Charibert, King of Paris, was a Christian who used the Church of St. Martin as her place of worship, and she had a bishop with her as her spiritual guide. The mission of Augustine was, needless to say, successful, and, though Christianity had its setbacks in this and other neighbouring kingdoms, it was in due course established in most parts of the South and Southeast.

Meanwhile Æthelfrith was king of the combined kingdoms of Northumbria until in 616 he was slain by Rædwald, King of East Anglia, at whose court Edwin had been living and who was now supporting Edwin's cause. Edwin, a son of King Ælle, belonged to the Deiran royal

---
[4] *HE*, I, 23.

family, and was therefore a rival of Æthelfrith. He had spent his early years in exile, at first with the Britons in North Wales and later with Rædwald. Here in Rædwald's court, as the finds at Sutton Hoo have proved,[5] civilization was of a high standard and European art and culture were familiar. Edwin must have known much about Christianity if he was really at the court of Cadfan in North Wales, as British tradition asserts;[6] while Rædwald had also accepted the new religion, though he afterwards relapsed into a sort of semi-heathenism.

Edwin, having gained the throne, was determined to make himself a king after the heroic type; but his knowledge of southern European culture made him eager to be something more. He succeeded his patron Rædwald as overlord of the whole of Britain with the exception of Kent—the fifth of the series of seven overlords whom Bede names in his *Ecclesiastical History*.[7] It was part of Edwin's ambition to ally himself to a court that stood also for southern culture and had associations with Rome; this was why he asked for the hand of Æthelburh, daughter of Æthelberht of Kent. She was granted to him on condition that she be allowed to keep her Christian faith; to this end she brought with her the Roman Paulinus, a member not of the original Augustinian mission but of the second party of four which arrived in England in 601. Not until late in 625 did he arrive with Edwin's bride in Northumbria. It was more than eighteen months before Edwin finally

---

[5] For a preliminary report see *The Sutton Hoo Burial*, published by the British Museum (London, 1947). A complete account of these astonishing finds is in course of preparation.

[6] This tradition is preserved only in a twelfth-century Life of St. Oswald. See *Symeon of Durham*, ed. T. Arnold (*RS*, LXXV) I, 345.

[7] *HE*, II, 5.

Historical Background

made up his mind to become a Christian and to be baptized at York on Easter Eve, 627. Among those who were baptized with him was his great-niece Hild, who was afterwards to become the first abbess of the monastery at Whitby.[8]

Edwin's reign was extremely prosperous while it lasted, and Bede describes with enthusiasm the peace that prevailed in Britain wherever his dominion reached, and his majestic progresses through his kingdom.[9] But it was not to last, for Bede ends his second book with an account of his overthrow by the combined force of Cædwalla (or Cadwallon), King of Gwynedd, and Penda of Mercia at the Battle of Hatfield Chase in 633. Edwin and his son Osfrith were killed. His enemies followed up their victory by a calculated devastation of all Northumbria. Paulinus fled, taking with him the widowed Queen Æthelburh and her two young children, one of whom, Eanflæd, was later destined to become Abbess of Whitby.

For a whole year Northumbria seemed to have returned to its old paganism. Once again it fell apart into its separate divisions of Bernicia and Deira. It was left to the warrior saint, Oswald, son of King Æthelfrith, to restore Christianity. Although Oswald was the son of Edwin's sister, Edwin had regarded him as a rival, for Oswald was the heir to the throne of Bernicia; so both Oswald and his brother Oswiu spent their youth in exile and received Christian teaching from the monks of Iona, the Irish monastery off the southwest coast of Scotland. At the battle of Heavenfield in 634 the British king Cadwallon was killed, the invaders were driven out, and the two king-

---
[8] *HE*, II, 14; IV, 23.
[9] *HE*, II, 16.

doms were united again under the rule of Oswald. Oswald at once set about re-establishing Christianity with the help of St. Aidan, an Irish monk from Iona, who naturally introduced the practices and liturgy of the Irish Church.

The Christianity of the British Church was very naturally suspect so far as the Saxon invaders were concerned, no attempt having been made by the Britons to convert their conquerors. But the Irish had always been on friendlier terms with those invaders, for they had never been subject to their cruel ravages. Hence Oswald had no trouble in getting help from the Irish for the reconversion of the Northumbrian kingdom. St. Aidan set up his diocesan centre at Lindisfarne, accessible only at low tide and isolated enough to give Aidan and his monks the remoteness that the Irish monastics loved, but within easy access of Bamborough, where Oswald had his fort residence. The King and the Bishop worked together and succeeded in re-establishing the church on more solid foundations than Paulinus and his helpers had been able to build. Unfortunately Oswald was killed in battle in 642, while fighting against Penda of Mercia, his heathen foe, who was to be a constant thorn in the side of Northumbria for thirteen years. Oswald died praying for his followers. In fact, " 'May God have mercy on their souls,' as Oswald said when he fell to the ground,"[10] afterwards became a proverbial expression.

After Oswald's death the kingdom once more was divided up into its two parts, Oswald's brother Oswiu assumed the throne of Bernicia, while a young man of the royal house of Deira, Oswine, a great-nephew of King

---

[10] *HE*, III, 12.

Historical Background

Ælle, became ruler of that kingdom but still retained the friendship of St. Aidan. He was an earnest Christian, but his reign was destined to be a short one. Oswiu was ambitious and was determined to become ruler of the whole of Northumbria. First of all, he married Eanflæd, who as a child of ten had been taken by Paulinus to Kent, where she grew up. As Eanflæd was a daughter of Edwin, this marriage gave him a claim to the throne of Deira. But meanwhile Penda of Mercia was growing more and more powerful and becoming Oswiu's greatest rival. Oswiu knew it was only a matter of time before Penda leapt. So, perhaps to gain extra power, he invaded Deira in 651 and put Oswine to flight, afterwards causing him to be murdered in cold blood. He got little good out of this action, however, for the Deirans chose as ruler a son of Oswald, Œthelwald, who speedily put himself under the protection of Penda. Aidan survived his friend Oswine by only a few days.[11]

After a few years of uneasy peace, Penda made up his mind to destroy Oswiu. Bede tells us that Oswiu made an attempt to buy Penda off but was finally compelled to fight for existence. He was surrounded by enemies. His nephew Œthelwald was willing to help the enemy all he could, even though he refrained from going into the fight himself, possibly fearing the greatest calamity that could befall a Germanic warrior, that of killing a near kinsman either accidentally or deliberately. Also fighting for Penda was Æthelhere, King of the East Angles, who is referred to by Bede as *"auctor ipse belli,"* whatever that may mean.[12]

---
[11] *HE*, III, 17.
[12] *HE*, III, 24. The Old English translation reads *ordfruma* for *auctor*, meaning "source" or "origin."

Oswiu's old British foes combined against him while his own son Ecgfrith was a hostage at Penda's court. The battle was fought in 655 at an unidentified river, the Winwæd, somewhere in the Leeds district. It resulted in a great victory for Oswiu. Penda and Æthelhere were both killed.

Oswiu's victory had many important results. It established his rule over Deira and gave the deathblow to heathenism in the Midlands. Through it Oswiu became overlord not only of the Mercians but of all the peoples of southern England. But this did not last long, for soon afterwards Penda's son, Wulfhere, gained the throne of Mercia, and after 658 he gradually made himself supreme over southern England and forced Oswiu to confine his influence to the area north of the river Humber.

Another important result of the battle was the fulfilment of the vow which Oswiu made before the battle, that if he were successful he would dedicate his baby daughter, Ælfflæd, to the Lord and give twelve small estates on which to build monasteries, six in Bernicia and six in Deira. Ælfflæd was put under the care of St. Hild, whose subsequent career will concern us later.

Meanwhile Oswiu continued to reign successfully in Northumbria and the time began for a fresh and very important series of journeys to Rome which were to alter the whole face of Northumbria, in fact of Western Europe. These journeys are connected with the names of two young men, Biscop Baducing, later known as Benedict Biscop, and Wilfrid, a youth of noble birth who had been brought up in Lindisfarne and was a protégé of Oswiu's queen, Eanflæd. The Queen, who had been educated under the influence of Paulinus and was entirely devoted to the Roman form of worship, was much interested in Wilfrid's

Historical Background

desire to go to Rome and may well have had something to do with Biscop Baducing's determination to go. With the help of her cousin Eorcenberht, King of Kent, the two young men started off together for Rome in 653.[13] Benedict returned home some time before Wilfrid. When the latter got back about 658, his enthusiastic description of all he had seen and learned filled Alhfrith, the sub-king of Deira and son of Oswiu, with such fervour that in due course he and Alhfrith managed to persuade Oswiu to call the Council of Whitby, a gathering of kings, bishops, and priests, which in 664 accepted the Roman allegiance and so brought the Northumbrian Church into the main stream of Roman culture.[14] When in 665 Benedict Biscop went to Rome again, Alhfrith would have gone with him if Oswiu had not forbidden it. But meanwhile Wilfrid remained and in 664 there was a vacancy in the see. This happened because the Irish bishop Colman left, refusing to accept the Roman allegiance, and his successor Tuda died suddenly of the plague soon after the Council. So, at the age of thirty, Wilfrid was consecrated bishop of the whole realm, having his diocesan seat at York. Though Wilfrid had many difficulties and spent only twenty of the forty-six years of his episcopacy ruling his see, yet by his journeys to Rome and his appeals to the Apostolic See, he brought the North into close contact with the papal court; he built churches at Ripon, Hexham, and York which were as fine as any in Western Europe, and he exercised a great influence on the learning, art, and architecture of his time. He is also generally credited with the introduction of the Benedictine Rule in the North.[15]

---

[13] *Eddius*, c. 3.
[14] *HE*, III, 25; *Eddius*, c. 10.
[15] *Eddius*, c. 14.

An equally close bond was created by Benedict Biscop, who during the reign of Oswiu made two more visits to Rome and finally brought back Theodore of Tarsus, the newly consecrated Archbishop of Canterbury, who was to play an important part in refashioning the English Church and bringing it still more closely into contact with Rome. One of his first journeys was to the North, where he reconsecrated Chad, who had been consecrated by British bishops and who was acting as bishop in Wilfrid's place, as Bishop of York, having been appointed by Oswiu while Wilfrid was in Gaul. Theodore restored Wilfrid to his rightful position and soon afterwards Oswiu died, in 670.

During the twenty-seven years of his reign, Oswiu had seen Christianity firmly established. He was succeeded by his son Ecgfrith, who, a few years before, had married Æthelthryth, better known as St. Audrey or St. Etheldreda. She was the daughter of Anna, King of the East Angles. Not long afterwards, encouraged by St. Wilfrid, she left her husband before the consummation of their marriage, entering the double monastery of Coldingham, which was ruled over by Æbbe, Ecgfrith's aunt. Wilfrid had been on friendly terms with Ecgfrith until this happening, for which Ecgfrith never forgave him. When he married his second wife, Iurminburg, sister-in-law of Centwine, King of Wessex, trouble quickly arose. So when Theodore and Ecgfrith agreed that Wilfrid's great diocese should be divided into three parts, the Bishop refused to accept their decision and in 679 went to Rome to appeal to the Pope. He returned in 680 with the papal judgment. Even though this was a compromise, Ecgfrith refused to accept it and, after imprisoning Wilfrid for a time, finally expelled him altogether.[16]

---

[16] *Eddius*, c. 34.

Historical Background

But though Ecgfrith was opposed to Wilfrid, he was by no means opposed to Roman culture and arts. When in 674 Benedict Biscop came back from his fourth visit to Rome laden with books and treasures, Ecgfrith gave him 50 hides of land on the north bank of the mouth of the river Wear. Here Benedict built a church of stone and even put glass in the windows,[17] being assisted by Gaulish workmen. Benedict Biscop was so pleased about all this that he went to Rome for a fifth visit, taking his friend Ceolfrith with him, in order to collect books, relics, and paintings for the monastery. Ecgfrith was greatly impressed and so in 681 gave land for another monastery at Jarrow, about six miles away. Thither Ceolfrith was transferred with twenty-two of the brethren, ten monks and twelve novices, one of them almost certainly the eight-year-old Bede, who during his lifetime was to make the monastery famous all over Western Europe. Jarrow was really an extension of the Wearmouth monastery, as the double dedication of the two churches, to St. Peter and St. Paul, St. Peter at Wearmouth and St. Paul at Jarrow, was intended to show.[18]

Very soon afterwards Benedict went again to Rome for the sixth and last time; in 684, the year before the Jarrow church was dedicated, he returned with books, paintings, and relics to supply the needs of the new monastery. In fact, as Bede himself says of Benedict, "He visited lands overseas so many times in order that we might rest quietly within the cloisters and yet have an abundant feast of salu-

---

[17] The recent excavations on the site made by Miss Rosemary Cramp of Durham University have revealed the remains of a great hall with Roman pavement and considerable quantities of seventh-century coloured glass of Gaulish type.

[18] *HAB*, cc. 4, 7: Plummer, I, 367-71.

tary learning."[19] Ceolfrith, the first Abbot of Jarrow, also did his share in increasing the libraries and we are even told that he doubled the number of books at both Wearmouth and Jarrow, though Bede, who makes this statement, does not say how.[20] Probably some of the MSS were those he brought from Rome and others may have been the MSS copied under his direction; for it was under him that the three famous Pandects, or copies of the whole Bible, were produced, of which the Codex Amiatinus, now in Florence, was one.[21]

After the Council of Whitby, the monastery of Lindisfarne had been in the charge of Eata of Melrose and later of Cuthbert, both of whom had accepted the Roman allegiance. The division of the diocese had created bishoprics both at Hexham and Lindisfarne. Cuthbert, though he became Prior of Lindisfarne, was a recluse at heart, and at last achieved his ambition and from 673 to 685 lived as a hermit on a remote island called Farne, off the Northumbrian coast and nine miles away across the North Sea from Lindisfarne. But in 685 he was compelled, against his will, to become Bishop of Hexham and then, by exchange with his old master Eata, Bishop of Lindisfarne, and for two years he carried out his duties conscientiously.[22]

The year 685 was an important one in the history of the North. One of the first of Cuthbert's tasks after his consecration was to visit Carlisle and there, while examining the extensive Roman remains of the city, he had a vision of Ecgfrith's death. The King was killed at Nechtansmere

---

[19] Homelia, I, 13: *Corpus Christianorum Series Latina*, CXXII, 93.
[20] *HAB*, c. 15: Plummer, I, 379.
[21] *HAB*, c. 17: Plummer, I, 381.
[22] *VP*, c. 24: *Two Lives*, p. 238.

Historical Background

with all his bodyguard while fighting against the Picts, commanded by his cousin, their king, Bruide mac Beli. Bede declares, quoting Virgil, that from this time the strength of Northumbria began to "ebb and fall away."[23]

The death of King Ecgfrith removed one of the most determined of Wilfrid's foes. Aldfrith, the illegitimate son of Oswiu by an Irish princess, succeeded to the throne of the combined kingdoms of Deira and Bernicia. He was long remembered in Ireland as a poet, though none of his poems has survived. He gave up all idea of further conquest and devoted himself to internal affairs. The twenty years of his reign (685-705) cover one of the most brilliant periods in the history of the North. Literature, painting, building, sculpture, and other arts flourished. It is likely that vernacular literature flourished at the court too. Wilfrid came north again in 686 at the request of Archbishop Theodore and, for a brief period, he ruled all the Northumbrian dioceses except for Lindisfarne, which Cuthbert still ruled. Cuthbert died in 687 and his body was buried in Lindisfarne. For a year Wilfrid took over his diocese too, and it seems to have been a very troubled time, judging from Bede's comments. But then St. John of Beverley took over the Hexham diocese and Eadberht, a learned and holy priest, replaced Cuthbert. Wilfrid was unable to remain at peace even with Aldfrith and by 692 he had been banished again. Meanwhile Aldfrith continued his peaceful and happy reign. He kept his kingdom intact, and Western civilization owes him a debt of gratitude because he refused to be embroiled like Oswiu and Ecgfrith in outside warlike activities. So learning and culture flourished until after his death in 705.[24]

---

[23] *HE*, IV, 26.
[24] Cf. Stenton, pp. 88 ff.

As for the rest of the kingdoms, Mercia, after its revolt against Oswiu about 658, supplanted Northumbria, becoming supreme in southern England by the efforts of its king, Wulfhere. The reign of his brother Æthelred was not marked by any conquests, and his kingdom was less than that of Wulfhere, though he seems to have ruled over a territory stretching to the west as far as the British kingdoms of Powys and Gwynedd in North Wales, and to the south towards the country about the middle and upper Thames, Lindsey having been recovered from Northumbria in 678. Æthelred was a pious king, though Bede tells us that in 676 he made an attack on Kent and ravaged churches and monasteries there.[25] He retired in 704 to the monastery at Bardney in Lincolnshire, of which he was a benefactor if not the founder. His wife Osthryth was a daughter of King Oswiu. On his abdication, Cenred, his nephew, became king and ruled until 709, when he went as a pilgrim to Rome, accompanied by a young man called Offa, son of the king of Essex, of whom we know nothing except that he was so lovable and handsome that the whole East Saxon race longed for him to succeed to the throne. The incident was considered important enough to obtain a mention in the *Liber Pontificalis*.[26] Cenred and Offa became monks, and both, according to the entry in the same book, died soon afterwards.[27] When Cenred resigned, Æthelred's son, Ceolred, succeeded and proved himself to be but a poor ruler, bringing down on himself the condemnation of St. Boniface; even Eddius hints at his unruly conduct.[28] He seems to have died insane in 716. He was

---

[25] *HE*, IV, 12.
[26] Cf. W. Levison, "Bede as a Historian," *BLTW*, p. 120.
[27] *Liber Pontificalis, Vita Constantini*, c. 9 (ed. Mommsen, p. 225).
[28] Tangl, No. 73, pp. 152-53; *Eddius*, c. 64, p. 139.

Historical Background

succeeded by Æthelbald, who, like Offa his successor, calls himself *"rex Anglorum"* in his charters, and in at least one charter is called *"rex non solum Marcersium sed et omnium provinciarum quae generale nomine Sutangli dicuntur."*[29] At the height of his power he was, as Stenton points out, "head of a confederation which included Kent, Wessex and every other kingdom between the Humber and the Channel."[30] After a reign of forty-one years he was murdered by his bodyguard at Seckington near Tamworth.

In East Anglia, after the time of Rædwald things did not go well. The magnificent court, whose splendour is reflected in the Sutton Hoo discoveries of 1939, seems to have been reduced by a long series of calamities to the position of a subject state. Rædwald's two sons, Rægenhere and Eorpwald, were both killed. Rægenhere fell at the Battle of the Idle, when his father won the victory which put Edwin on the throne of Northumbria; Eorpwald was murdered apparently because he embraced the Christian faith. The swift rise to power of Penda of Mercia was disastrous for East Anglia. Three of their kings were slain fighting against him—Sigeberht, Ecgric, and Anna—while King Æthelhere was killed fighting as Mercia's ally against Oswiu of Northumbria. There followed a period during which comparative peace reigned; although they were a subject race, the East Anglians had only three kings in nearly a hundred years—Æthelwald (655-664), Aldwulf (664-713), and Ælfwald (713-749). It is their Christianity rather than their power that Bede emphasizes, though two of Anna's daughters married royal princes; Æthelthryth married no less a person than Ecgfrith of Northumbria,

---
[29] *EHD I*, 453.
[30] Stenton, p. 202. Cf. *HE*, V, 23.

and Sexburh married Eorcenberht, King of Kent and grandson of the Æthelberht who had received Augustine and his band. Æthelthryth, as we have seen, left her husband to enter a monastery and in due course returned to Ely to establish a double community of monks and nuns, while Sexburh, after her sister's death in 680, became abbess of the Ely monastery and about 695 was responsible for the translation of her sister's uncorrupt body, of which Bede gives a very vivid account.[31] Æthelburh, another daughter of Anna, became abbess of a monastery in Faremoûtiers-en-Brie in Gaul, also a double community. Fursa, an Irish monk, with several companions also came to East Anglia, where they were given a site to build a monastery in the ruins of Burgh Castle.[32]

Of seventh-century Essex little is known; its importance as a dependent kingdom seems to have been small, but it had one interesting link with Northumbria in that Cedd, brother of St. Chad, was sent by Oswiu to help the recently baptized King Sigeberht in the evangelization of the kingdom, though Cedd seems to have had no see. He founded two monasteries, one at Bradwell-on-Sea, where an ancient church, probably of Cedd's time, still survives,[33] and the other at Tilbury. He was often in Northumbria and, with the help of his brother Chad, founded a monastery at Lastingham in Yorkshire. His last activity was to come to the Council of Whitby (664), where he acted as interpreter for the Irish party. He died of the plague soon afterwards and was buried at Lastingham.

---

[31] *HE*, IV, 19.
[32] *HE*, III, 19.
[33] Taylor, I, 91.

Historical Background

In Northumbria the successor to St. Cuthbert in the diocese of Lindisfarne, Eadberht, continued his quiet life, marked by only one outstanding event, the elevation of the relics of St. Cuthbert, whose cult as a saint was already established and rapidly growing. The elevation took place on 20 March, 698. His body was found as undecayed as when it was buried. The outer vestments and shoes were removed, and the body was wrapped in a new garment and put into a new coffin. Remains of all these are still preserved in Durham Cathedral.[34]

Bishop Eadberht himself died six weeks after this event and was buried in the tomb from which Cuthbert's body had been removed. His successor, Eadfrith, is remembered as the artist bishop who was responsible, at any rate for the most part, for the illumination and the copying of the magnificent Lindisfarne Gospels which are preserved in the British Museum.[35] When he died in 721, he was buried near St. Cuthbert. The remains of both these bishops, together with St. Cuthbert's relics, were removed in 875 owing to the depredations of the Viking hordes. They were taken first to Chester-le-Street and later on, about 995, to Durham.[36]

With the death of Aldfrith in 705 the greatness of Northumbria slowly declined. Osred, son of Aldfrith, came to the throne at the age of eight and was killed in 716 at the age of nineteen, after a precociously dissolute life. With Ceolred of Mercia he received a bitter reproof

---

[34] *The Relics of St. Cuthbert*, ed. C. F. Battiscombe, pp. 35 ff.
[35] See *Codex Lindisfarnensis*, ed. R. L. S. Bruce-Mitford and T. J. Brown (Olten and Lausanne, 1960).
[36] *Symeon of Durham, Historia Dunelmensis Ecclesiae III, 1*; ed. T. Arnold, I, 78 ff.

from St. Boniface.[37] He was succeeded by Cenred and then Osric, both of whom had short and stormy reigns. They were succeeded by Ceolwulf, to whom Bede dedicated his *History*. But even before the book was finished, it is clear that Bede had doubts about the future;[38] nor is it surprising, considering that in 731 Ceolwulf was taken and forcibly tonsured by his undisciplined followers. Bede died in 735, and two years later Ceolwulf resigned his throne and spent the rest of his life in the monastery at Lindisfarne. He was succeeded in 737 by Eadberht, son of Eata and brother of Archbishop Egbert of York, the friend and disciple of Bede. His reign of twenty-one years was looked upon as a golden age by Alcuin, who grew up as a schoolboy at York during this period, studying in the cathedral school under Egbert, who had founded it, and later under Egbert's kinsman Æthelberht, who himself became archbishop in 767. King Eadberht was a friend of Pippin, King of the Franks. In 758 he resigned and became a monk at York, and almost at once the Northumbrian kingdom fell into confusion from which it never recovered. Learning continued to flourish during the greater part of this period at Wearmouth and Jarrow, at Lindisfarne, Hexham, York, and Whitby; but by the end of the eighth century the Scandinavian raids began, and the savage barbarities of the invaders reduced the monasteries to shadows of their former selves. Yet their influence lived on for centuries, so that when these great monasteries of the Northeast were little more than a heap of ruins, the disciples of the men who had been trained in them and the works that had been written there did much to mould the future history of Western Europe.

---

[37] Tangl, No. 73, pp. 152-53.
[38] *HE*, V, 23.

II. GREGORY THE GREAT

GREGORY THE GREAT was a greatly beloved and honoured figure in England all through the Middle Ages. Even in Bede's time there were at least three altars dedicated to him, in Canterbury, York, and Whitby, and it would be surprising if there were no more.[1] The fact that one of the earliest pieces of writing which have survived from Anglo-Saxon times was concerned with his life is in itself a tribute to the love and affection in which his name was held. He is referred to by our author as "our own St. Gregory," "our holy teacher," "our blessed master," "this apostolic saint of ours," and we are told that "in the Day of Judgment he will bring us, the English race whom he has taught, to present them to the Lord."[2] Nor was our author alone in yielding honour to Gregory. Bede in his *Ecclesiastical History* devotes one of his longest chapters to an account of his life,[3] while Aldhelm and Alcuin also speak of him with affection.[4] At the synod of *Cloveshoe* in 747 it was declared that March 12, the day of Gregory's death, was to be celebrated in all churches and monasteries.[5]

Gregory was born in Rome about the year 540 of a wealthy senatorial family. His father Gordianus and his mother Sylvia were both earnest Christians, while two of his aunts lived under a strict religious rule in their own house. Later on, Gregory had portraits of his father and mother made which were seen and described by John the

---
[1] C. 19 below; *HE*, II, 3, 20.
[2] Cc. 4, 5, 6, 27, and 30 below.
[3] *HE*, II, 1.
[4] Aldhelm, *De laude virginitatis*, c. 55: MGH *Auct. ant.*, XV, 314. Alcuin, *MGH Epp.*, IV, 182.
[5] Haddan and Stubbs, *Councils and Ecclesiastical Documents*, III, 368.

Deacon, Gregory's biographer, in the ninth century. They hung in the house where Gregory was brought up, on the Caelian Hill, which was afterwards to become the monastery of St. Andrew.[6]

Gregory's youth must have been a troubled one, for Rome changed hands no less than four times while he was a boy. Totila, King of the Goths, captured it in 546; then it was restored and rewon by Belisarius, only to be captured again by Totila in 549 and then won back in 552 by Narses for the Emperor Justinian. The latter remained in control until his death in 565. The boy was educated in Rome in spite of all these difficulties, but one cannot help suspecting that his formal education was somewhat sketchy. It is clear, for instance, that he knew no Greek.[7] Life was very difficult and the brutality of the Goths was only equalled by the commanders of the Emperor, especially Narses, whose behaviour caused so much trouble among the Italians that he was finally recalled to Constantinople.

Next came the growing threat of the great Germanic nation, the Lombards. They descended upon Italy in 568, when Gregory was already in his later twenties and, from then on, the threat became ever greater. Though we know little of his earlier years it is clear that he became recognized more and more as a public figure and one who might hope to play an important part in leading the troubled land to a more lasting peace. So in 573 he was appointed Prefect of the city, his duties being to superintend its financial affairs, watch over its buildings and its policing, provide food for the inhabitants, and preside over the senate. With the Lombards gradually encroaching upon their

---

[6] John the Deacon's *Life*, IV, 83: *PL*, LXXV, 229.
[7] Cf. *MGH Epp.*, I, 476; II, 258, 330.

domains, it seemed to many citizens as though Imperial Rome was nearing its end.

Not long after assuming the rank of prefect Gregory came to a serious decision. His father was dead, and his mother had retired to spend the rest of her years in prayer: so all the family inheritance came to him. He thereupon built and endowed six monasteries on his estate in Sicily; he reserved a small sum with which to convert his home on the Caelian Hill into a monastery, and the rest he gave to the poor. Then having disposed of his entire estate, he entered the monastery which he had dedicated, fittingly enough, to St. Andrew and became, not its first abbot but a simple monk in 574, just about the time that Benedict I became Pope.

These were happy years for Gregory, perhaps his happiest; and it was during this period that the incident may have happened when he met the Anglian youths who aroused in his mind a strong desire to go as a missionary to the distant land from which these lads had come. But it was not to be, and about 578 Benedict I took Gregory from his cell to make him Seventh Deacon, whose duty was to assist the Pope's charitable labours in one of the seven districts into which Rome was divided for this purpose. Soon afterwards Benedict died and his successor, Pelagius II, found himself expected to help the citizens of Rome, who were in the last stages of distress and terror, with the Lombard armies pressing at their gates and famine threatening. Pelagius decided that it was necessary to keep in touch with the Emperor Tiberius II, who had lately succeeded to full power as Emperor in Constantinople, after the death of Justin. He must be kept informed of the state of affairs in Rome and, if possible, persuaded to give help, both in

men and money, to save Rome. So Gregory was sent because it was felt that no one was better able than he to put the case of the distressed Romans before the Emperor. He represented the Pope and was given the official title of "apocrisarius."[8]

Gregory lived for close on seven years in Constantinople and seems to have been very unhappy in the secular employment and worldly business which occupied the greater part of his attention. His only alleviation he found in the company of several of his fellow-monks from the Caelian Hill who accompanied him and, through their encouragement and example, he gained fresh strength and courage, binding himself, as he says, "as it were by an anchor cable to the calm shores of prayer while being tossed about by the ceaseless tide of secular affairs."[9] Two matters helped to occupy his mind and give him the encouragement he needed. One sprang from the presence of Leander, afterwards Bishop of Seville, who together with some of his monks was living in retirement in Constantinople because Visigothic politics had made his further presence in Spain inexpedient. Leander and his companions urged Gregory to undertake an exposition of the Book of Job. This proved to be a lengthy task and was not finished until some years later. It consisted of thirty-five books and is often known as the *Moralia*. It expounded the book in accordance with the theological practice of the times under three headings relating to its historic, its moral, and its allegorical meaning. The other matter which occupied him during his stay

---
[8] Du Cange defines the word as the name of a messenger or ambassador who carried the answers of their chiefs. An alternative word was *responsalis*. It was used by the papal see as the name of the official who represented the Pope at Constantinople. See Plummer, II, 69.

[9] See c. 2 below and notes.

Gregory the Great

was a disputation with Eutychius, Patriarch of Constantinople, who taught that the resurrected body of the believer would be impalpable and more subtle than wind or air. This Gregory stoutly denied, basing his proofs on Scripture, and so violent grew the argument that the Emperor Tiberius had to take a hand and, finally, after hearing both parties separately, came down on the side of Gregory and ordered the Patriarch's book to be burned. Gregory and Eutychius took to their beds after the dispute was over. Eutychius in fact died, having renounced his heretical views shortly before his death.[10] Very soon afterwards, in 582, Tiberius died too, and his place was taken by his general, Maurice, who was also his stepson.

In 585 Gregory was recalled to Rome by Pope Pelagius II and re-entered his monastery but this time as its abbot. It was a period of great peril, for although Rome had not actually fallen to the Lombards the prospects seemed very dark. To add to the general turmoil, in 589 the Tiber overflowed its banks, doing great destruction to many buildings and bringing in its train an outbreak of plague, in the course of which Pelagius died (January, 590).

At that point the clergy and people alike realized that there was only one man who could cope with the situation. The Pope was not simply a spiritual leader; in those times he had also to be a man of practical insight and political ability. Because he had these capacities the whole community believed that Gregory was the most suitable candidate for the honour; and in addition he had had good experience as a diplomat. Our author describes Gregory's almost frantic attempts to avoid the honour that the whole populace wished to force upon him. But once he realized that

---

[10] See *DCB*, II, 414, *s.v. Eutychius*.

his appointment to the vacant papacy was inevitable, Gregory set about his task with courage and resolution. He called for a great act of repentance and assembled all the inhabitants in seven companies, one at the principal church in each of the seven regions of Rome, and made them march in procession, chanting litanies, to the Church of S. Maria Maggiore.

One of the chief primary sources of our knowledge of Gregory's life and character is his correspondence,[11] much of which has been preserved and which provides us with a very full record of his papal career, as well as being an admirable historical source for the political and economic background and for the religious and intellectual life of the times. His letters also form the primary source of information about the Anglo-Saxon mission. Bede, at some time during his writing of the *Ecclesiastical History*, obtained copies of some of them and introduced them into his work, but our biographer does not seem to have known of them. They reveal the character of the Pope himself, his deep spiritual life as well as his wide and comprehensive knowledge of the world, and a realistic insight into the actual conditions of his times and what was needed for the future. He had what all the great men of history have possessed, bold initiative and boundless energy. While still a young man, he seems to have realized that the imposing structure built by his forefathers—a soulless organization supported mainly by brute force—was doomed to fall. It was gradually borne in upon him that amid all this welter of destruction the only solid rock was that on which Christ had founded his Church. The new attitude which he brought to the Papacy was a conscious turning towards the

---

[11] Edited by P. Ewald and L. M. Hartmann. *MGH Epp.,* I and II.

Germanic nations that promised very soon to be the masters of Western Europe. He hears with delight through his friend Leander of the conversion of King Reccared of Spain from the Arian heresy. He writes to Reccared in the somewhat fulsome style that he so often adopted in writing to great princes, "What shall I say at the dread judgment to that great Judge if I come empty-handed while you bring with you a great flock of believers won to the true faith by your earnest and constant teaching?"[12] Yet he warns him as he so often warns his correspondents against the sin of pride at his success.

In the Frankish kingdom he had much to contend with: simony and superstition in the Church and the unwillingness of the ecclesiastical authorities to interfere. The brutality and evil living of the rulers was an additional trial: though it is sometimes difficult to understand Gregory's almost fulsome flattery of Brunhild and her grandsons Theudebert and Theoderic or of Childebert II of Austrasia or Chlotar II of Neustria, all of them, especially Brunhild, notoriously cruel and evil-living. Gregory, however, was biased by the fact that the Franks were Catholics and ardent supporters of their faith against the Arian heresy long held by the Ostrogoths, the Visigoths, and other Germanic peoples.

But it is clear that the English mission kept a very high place in his thoughts and wishes. He seems to have had a kind of foresight of the part that the distant isle was to play in the future history of the Church. Here was a people to be won, a people not yet trapped by the heresy of Arianism but just simple heathen and ready to be led to the true Catholic faith by the preaching of the Gospel. His

---

[12] *MGH Epp.*, II, 222.

letters show the care with which he watched over the mission, sending the prior of his own monastery as their head, encouraging them with his sympathy when they lost heart, writing letters of commendation to no less than eight Frankish monarchs and bishops through whose kingdoms and provinces their way led. He must have received good news of the mission very soon, for in July, 598, he wrote to Bishop Eulogius, Patriarch of Alexandria, telling him that Augustine had baptized no less than ten thousand Englishmen *(Angli)* at the previous Christmas festival, only a matter of months after the missionaries had arrived.[13] He does not state specifically that the King of Kent was among the number baptized, but by June, 601, he is writing a series of letters connected with the new church, one to Bertha, King Æthelberht's consort, urging her to encourage her husband in his task of spreading Christianity and another to the King to the same effect, urging him to suppress idolatry in the land and to follow the teachings of Augustine. He also sends the archbishop's pallium to Augustine, bidding him appoint a metropolitan in York with twelve suffragan bishops and make his see in London and appoint twelve other suffragans for himself. Clearly, in taking this step Gregory was looking forward too far, for, owing to the apostasy of Essex, which drove out its bishop, Mellitus, about 617, it did not have another bishop until 664, when the archbishop's see was firmly established in Canterbury. He also sent by Laurentius, Justus, and Mellitus answers to certain questions which Augustine had sent him. These answers, included in full by Bede in his *History*,[14] have given rise to much discussion, and their

---
[13] *MGH Epp.*, II, 31.
[14] *HE*, I, 27.

Gregory the Great 27

authenticity has been challenged by modern scholars, but without much evidence. They are known as the *Libellus Responsionum,* and a number of early manuscripts of the book still exist. Another letter, sent to Mellitus about the same time, contained instructions to Augustine on missionary methods which seem to contradict somewhat surprisingly the advice he had first given to Æthelberht—namely, that he should destroy the shrines and temples of the idols. But now he changed his mind, deciding that it would be better to destroy the idols and then reconsecrate their shrines, possibly feeling that the great numbers converted could not be dealt with if they proceeded with the drastic method of destroying the shrines completely and then building new churches sufficient in number and size for the great crowds of newly baptized converts to worship in.[15] Possibly he realized, as Plummer suggests,[16] that Æthelberht needed egging on and Augustine needed holding back. The other letter of this group is to Augustine, expressing his joy over the success of the mission but warning him that he must not be unduly elated by the miracles he was performing.[17]

In addition to the letters Gregory also sent various gifts of vestments and relics, as well as many manuscripts, the basis doubtless of the school at Canterbury later developed by Theodore and Hadrian. Of these manuscripts there are still a few possible survivors, such as the so-called Canterbury Gospels now in the Library of Corpus Christi College, Cambridge (C.C.C.C. 286), and the oldest copy of the Rule of St. Benedict (Oxford, Bodleian, Hatton 48

---
[15] *HE,* I, 30.
[16] Plummer, II, 58.
[17] *HE,* I, 31.

[3684]). Alfred the Great, writing some verses in praise of Gregory, states that Augustine brought a copy of the *Regula Pastoralis* to England with him.[18] It is therefore not surprising that the English should have had so enthusiastic a love for Gregory. Even if the story of his foiled attempt to head a mission to England, as told by our author, is only legend, at any rate, as Gregory himself said in his letter to Augustine and his faint-hearted companions, he would gladly have laboured with them in the conversion of this the outstanding part of the far-flung Germanic world that still remained heathen.

Bede was very familiar with Gregory's writings. He gives a list of his works[19] in which he includes the *Homilies on the Gospels*[20] and the *Homilies on Ezekiel*,[21] the *Libellus Responsionum*, which he quotes in full, the *Moralia*,[22] the *Regula Pastoralis*,[23] and the *Dialogues*.[24] So familiar is he with the latter that he frequently in his *History* works brief phrases from them into his narrative, especially in Books IV and V. In fact in these two books are at least fourteen phrases, usually only four or five words long, which are derived from the *Dialogues*. The Whitby monk is also familiar with the *Dialogues*, the *Moralia* or at any rate the prefatory letter to Leander, the *Regula Pastoralis*, the *Homilies on the Gospels*, and the *Homilies on Ezekiel*

---

[18] *EHD I*, 819. Cf. also K. Sisam, *Studies in the History of Old English Literature* (Oxford, 1953), p. 141.
[19] *HE*, II, 5.
[20] *PL*, LXXVI, 1075-1312.
[21] *PL*, LXXVI, 785-1072.
[22] *PB*, LXXV, 501-76, 782.
[23] *PL*, LXXVII, 13-128.
[24] Ed. U. Moricca. See Bibliography.

Gregory the Great 29

but does not seem to have known the *Libellus Responsionum.*

Of these writings, the *Moralia* or *Commentary on the Book of Job,* with its important autobiographical preface addressed to Leander, has already been described. The four books of *Dialogues,* written about 594, also with an autobiographical preface, were extremely popular throughout the Middle Ages.[25] They consist of narratives related by Gregory to his friend Peter the Deacon. The stories chiefly deal with miraculous happenings, while the second book relates the Life of St. Benedict of Nursia, our only source of information about that saint apart from what we learn from the Rule itself. The fourth book is concerned with visions of the afterlife; these visions, which spring from apocalyptic literature going back to the second century, acquired great popularity and throughout the Middle Ages such stories abounded, largely as the result of the popularity of this book. Visions of this kind are related by Bede, Felix, and Boniface in the eighth century, and the genre was to reach its climax in Dante's *Divine Comedy.*

The *Regula Pastoralis,* or *Pastoral Care,* was also a very popular book in England. Bede, writing to Egbert, Archbishop of York, urged him to make use of it, as well as the *Homilies on the Gospels,*[26] for his private meditations. Alcuin constantly recommended it and when writing to Eanbald II, a later Archbishop of York, urged him to take it with him wherever he went.[27] Alfred had it translated

---

[25] King Alfred ordered Bishop Wærferth to translate them into English about 891.
[26] *EHD* I, 736.
[27] Plummer, I, 406; *Alcuini Epistolae, MGH Epp.,* IV, 171. See also pp. 83, 166, 348, etc.

into English. The book contains wise counsels intended for those who were called to exercise the office of bishop. It is a book which had much influence all through the Middle Ages. It consists of four parts, the first two dealing with the qualities of mind and spirit after which the bishop should strive and the third being devoted to the art of preaching and the needs of different types of congregation. The brief fourth section emphasizes the necessity of humility on the part of the teacher.

Two series of Gregory's sermons have come down to us, one of forty homilies on the Gospel for the Day and another of twenty-two on the book of Ezekiel. These sermons, but especially the Ezekiel series, reflect the stormy background against which they were written. In one of the later sermons he says, "We see sorrows everywhere and hear laments. The towns are destroyed, the cities ruined, our fatherland is devastated. . . . Where is the state of Rome, once the mistress of the world? . . . Where is the senate? Where are the Romans? Their bones lie rotting and their flesh is consumed."[28] It was a hard and thankless task which Gregory had to face; he suffered from perpetual ill-health, like so many other great men who have left their mark on history. Often he longed for death and most of all for the contemplative life in the peace of his beloved monastery, but in spite of all this, though he saw the world in ruins around him, he knew what the future demanded— a new foundation on which to build a new empire and a new world; and in spite of all his physical disabilities he possessed the bold initiative and boundless energy required to carry out his plans. When he died in 604 he had, through

---

[28] *PL,* LXXVI, 1009-10. Quoted by E. S. Duckett, *The Gateway to the Middle Ages,* p. 563. A good modern account of St. Gregory will be found on pp. 531-612. See also cc. 23 and 26 below and notes.

his mission to the English, brought to pass one of the most decisive events in the history of the Western world. And not the least tribute to his greatness is that the first Life of him is this simple effort of an anonymous monk living in one of the remotest corners of the then known world, a place whose barbarous name Gregory had probably never heard, *Streoneshealh* in the kingdom of Deira. On behalf of the people whom Gregory had promised to snatch from the wrath of God to the true faith, the biographer offers this tribute, seeking, as he says, "to the best of my ability, to make mention of our master and write about him whom we with the rest of the world can call Saint Gregory."

III. WHITBY

ONE OF THE FIRST CONVERTS to be baptized by Paulinus with King Edwin on Easter Eve, 627, was the King's great-niece Hild. She was thirteen years old and daughter of Hereric, a grandson of King Ælle. Hereric, like his uncle Edwin, had been forced to go into exile for fear of Æthelfrith. He took refuge with his wife Bregoswith at the court of King Cerdic, or Ceretic, in Elmet, a British kingdom southwest of York, where his two children, Hereswith and Hild, were probably both born. Bede describes how, about the time of Hild's birth, Bregoswith had a dream. She fancied that her husband had been taken away from her and, search as she might, she could find no trace of him. But, during her search, she found a precious necklace under her robe, which, as she gazed closely at it, seemed to shine with a lustre that filled all Britain.[1] The necklace was a symbol of Hild; and since Bede tells us that Hereric was poisoned at Cerdic's court, one might con-

---
[1] *HE*, IV, 23.

clude from the story that Hild was a posthumous child. What happened to Bregoswith and her two children after her husband's death is not clear, but when Edwin, with the help of Rædwald, King of East Anglia, overthrew Æthelfrith in 616 at the Battle of the Idle and succeeded to the kingdom of Northumbria, Bregoswith probably joined him, about 617. Soon afterwards Edwin annexed the kingdom of Elmet and expelled Cerdic, possibly to avenge his nephew Hereric's death.

After Edwin's disastrous defeat and death in 633, possibly Hild and her mother found refuge in the court of the King of the East Angles. The family had close ties with the royal house of East Anglia, for Hild's sister, Hereswith, married a king of the East Angles, though Bede does not state his name.[2] She had a son, Aldwulf, who later became king, but some time before 647 she left her husband and took the veil, entering a monastery at Chelles near Paris.

It is not until 647, when Hild had reached the age of thirty-three, that we hear of her again. Her second cousin, King Oswald, had succeeded to the throne and in his turn been killed by Penda of Mercia in 642. His brother Oswiu had taken his place but had not yet become king of the whole of Northumbria but only of the more northerly part, the kingdom of Bernicia. At Oswald's court Hild would naturally have met St. Aidan, the Irish missionary whom Oswald had brought from Iona to assist him to reconvert the country to the Christianity that it had abandoned during the year 633-34. Hild was now seized with a desire to take the veil and so went down to the court of Anna, King of the East Angles, but only to find that her sister Here-

---

[2] F. M. Stenton, "The East Anglian Kings of the Seventh Century," *The Anglo-Saxons*, ed. P. Clemoes (London, 1959), pp. 43 ff.

swith had already gone to Chelles. She spent a year at the court, hoping to find an opportunity to rejoin her. But before she could set out, a message came from St. Aidan, recalling her to Northumbria. On her return he gave her a small piece of land on the north side of the river Wear. Here with a few companions she lived the monastic life for about a year. It seems to have been part of St. Aidan's plan to establish monasteries for women such as he had been familiar with in Ireland, where they had existed in some numbers in the sixth century.

The arrangement seems to have been only a temporary one, however, for not long afterwards Aidan sent Hild to replace a nun named Heiu, said to have been the first woman to take the monastic vows and habit in Northumbria. She too had been ordained by St. Aidan and was in charge of a double monastery of monks and nuns at Hartlepool. She went on to a site generally identified as Tadcaster, and Hild took her place at Hartlepool. Bede does not actually say it was a double monastery, but undoubtedly it was, because Oftfor, afterwards Bishop of the Hwicce, studied the Scriptures under Hild at "both her monasteries,"[3] which would mean Hartlepool and Whitby. Another important bit of evidence is that, during excavations on the site in 1833, memorial name slabs were discovered, carved with crosses and the names of the dead, both men and women, and dating from the seventh century.[4]

Meanwhile Penda of Mercia launched his attack on Oswiu and, as already described, was overwhelmed by Oswiu's army at the river Winwæd on November 15, 655.

---
[3] *HE*, IV, 23.
[4] G. Baldwin Brown, *Arts in Early England* (London, 1921), VI, 58-67.

As a result of a vow made before the battle, Oswiu gave his little daughter Ælfflæd into the charge of Hild at Hartlepool. Two years afterwards Hild was sent to Whitby to establish a monastery on one of the twelve estates which Oswiu had also vowed to give to the Lord if he was victorious. There Hild remained until her death in 680, and Ælfflæd was with her throughout the period.

Whitby is the Danish name of the place that Bede calls Streoneshealh. He explains the name as meaning *sinus fari*—"the bay of the lighthouse," which is not, so far as one can see, a translation of the Old English form; the meaning of the word is uncertain.[5] The monastery was situated on a cliff looking out to sea and the ruins of the medieval monastery and church later built on the site are still a landmark, visible miles away. Like Coldingham and Lindisfarne it was difficult of access, a feature shared by most of the monasteries of Irish antecedents. Modern excavations suggest that the earliest plan was of the Celtic type, with a rampart round it and a church in the center surrounded by a variety of buildings of wood or wattles and clay, intended as dormitories, refectories, kitchens, and guest-house with cells, possibly beehive-shaped, for the older monks.[6] It is not quite clear from Bede's account, however, whether Hild established an entirely new monastery or refounded an earlier one on the same site.

Whitby was perhaps the most famous example of the double monasteries of monks and nuns which seem to have arisen in Gaul in the seventh century. Aidan was probably

---

[5] *HE*, III, 25. See also *EHD, I*, 638, n. 2, and 640, n. 4.

[6] C. R. Peers and C. A. R. Radford, "The Saxon monastery at Whitby," *Archaeologia*, LXXXIX (1943), 27-88. See also J. Anderson, *Scotland in Early Christian Times* (Edinburgh, 1881), pp. 94 ff., and Lord Dunraven, *Notes on Irish Architecture,* ed. Margaret Stokes (London, 1875), I, 27 ff.

Whitby

responsible for the foundation of the double monasteries both at Hartlepool and Whitby, for, although this type of monastery did not originate in Ireland, it was at any rate known there.[7] The monks and nuns lived in separate quarters, though they worshipped together in the church. The monks would also act as resident chaplains, while there would perhaps be a number of lay brothers to do such work as could not be expected of a woman. In England the monasteries were under the rule of a woman, an abbess who was usually of royal birth like Hild. During the seventh century such double monasteries were also established at Coldingham, Barking, Ely, Bardney, Repton, Wimborne (Dorset), and Wenlock. Coldingham was the only place at which there was any breath of scandal; the story is told by Bede[8] in his account of Adamnan's vision and his prophecy of its destruction by fire, which took place about 685. At Whitby the double monastery included men students and presumably men teachers too.[9]

The importance of the monastery is emphasized by the fact that here in 664 was held the great Council which was to change completely the outlook of the Northumbrian Church. Oswiu here decided to accept the Roman discipline and to forsake the Irish practices such as the use of out-of-date cycles for the computation of the date of Easter, the form of tonsure which the Celtic clergy had insisted on retaining, and a variant method for the administration of baptism. Whitby's abbesses were associated with the royal houses of both Deira and Bernicia. And it was not unnatural that Oswiu should have chosen the monastery in

---

[7] Dom Louis Gougaud, *Christianity in Celtic Lands* (London, 1932), pp. 84 ff.

[8] *HE*, IV, 25.

[9] For a fuller account of these monasteries see *Two Lives*, p. 318 and refs.

which he had placed his own daughter. It was here too that his wife Eanflæd came after his death. Though she was a strong supporter of the Roman party, she, like the others, must have been influenced by memories of St. Aidan, even though Oswiu's conscience must have smitten him, too, since he had to bear the responsibility for the murder of Oswine, King of Deira and close friend of St. Aidan, thirteen years previously.[10]

At the Council it was the forcefulness of the young St. Wilfrid and the enthusiasm of Oswiu's son Alhfrith that won the day. Hild faithfully accepted the decisions of the Council, even though she opposed Wilfrid right up to the time of her death in 680.[11] It was not without significance that the church at Whitby was dedicated to St. Peter—a sign of the growing influence of the Roman party.

What Rule was observed in the monastery is not clear. Like all Rules in monasteries where Irish influence was felt, it was probably ascetic, though this side of it does not seem to have been stressed. All we know about it is that Hild established the same Rule at Whitby as had been observed at Hartlepool; the chief feature of this, Bede tells us, was her insistence on the Christian virtues of love, peace, and unity.[12] Life seems to have been strenuous and much time was spent in studying the Scriptures; judging by the Latinity of our author, the standard of Latin would not seem to have been very high, though his shortcomings may well be due to his own lack of ability. He was certainly competent in the Scriptures and was familiar with the works of Gregory; but whereas the anonymous writer

---

[10] *HE*, III, 14.
[11] *Eddius*, c. 54.
[12] *HE*, IV, 23.

at Lindisfarne who wrote a Life of St. Cuthbert at the turn of the seventh and eighth centuries knew the works of Athanasius, Sulpicius, Isidore, and Ambrose, our writer seems to know none of them.[13] He is familiar with that part of the *Liber Pontificalis* which dealt with Gregory and quotes from it; whether he possessed a complete copy is a matter of conjecture. He also had some knowledge of the works of St. Augustine and St. Jerome, though one cannot be sure whether his was a first-hand knowledge or whether he borrowed a quotation or two from elsewhere. It therefore seems unlikely that the Whitby library was as extensive as those at Wearmouth-Jarrow or at Lindisfarne. Hild's scholars were, however, in close touch with Canterbury and at least two of them, Oftfor[14] and John of Beverley,[15] also studied under Theodore of Tarsus, Archbishop of Canterbury; there is a possibility that this was a normal procedure for the Whitby-trained monks.

Altogether five of her pupils became bishops: Oftfor, who had studied with her at Hartlepool, and, after a time at Canterbury and later on at Rome, was consecrated by Wilfrid and went to assist Bosel, Bishop of the Hwicce; Bosa was consecrated Bishop of York by Theodore; John, better known as St. John of Beverley, became Bishop of Hexham and afterwards succeeded Bosa at York; Wilfrid, known as Wilfrid II, in his turn succeeded John as the last Bishop of York, for his successor Egbert received the pallium as the first archbishop. Of Ætla, Hild's fifth pupil, we know nothing except that he became Bishop of Dorchester. The see was of short duration, lasting only while the Mer-

---
[13] See below, p. 49.
[14] *HE*, IV, 23.
[15] *HE*, V, 3.

cians were in control of the area north of the upper Thames. From all this it would seem clear that the monastery contained its share of scholars and learned men.

It was before this company of learned men that Cædmon was brought.[16] He was a servant of the monastery and, judging by his name, had some strain of British descent. Bede's story of how he received the gift of poetical composition is one of the best-known episodes in the *Ecclesiastical History*, and it is for this incident that seventh-century Whitby is chiefly remembered. Bede claims that Cædmon was the first to use the traditional Old English metrical forms for composing religious as opposed to secular poetry. He was in due course received into the community, and Bede tells in considerable and enlightening detail the story of his last days.

Hild was taken ill about 674 and for over six years suffered from some kind of burning fever, perhaps ague. She continued her teaching work right up to the end and died on 17 May, 680. She was a remarkable woman and exercised a great influence on the Church of her day. Her mother's dream of the precious necklace and its wide-spreading lustre was not unduly exaggerated. "No woman," says Stenton, "in the middle ages ever held a position comparable with that of Hild of Whitby."[17] Bede evidently looked upon her with a deep respect and must have heard many stories about her, for Wearmouth was founded during her lifetime and Jarrow only a few years after her death. One interesting point which comes out in Bede's lengthy story of her death is the existence of a cell at Hackness, built in 680 about thirteen miles from Whitby and

---
[16] *HE*, IV, 24.
[17] Stenton, p. 162.

possibly intended as a place of retreat and rest for the Whitby sisters. The church there still shows traces of early Anglo-Saxon work.[18]

On her death she was succeeded by Ælfflæd, who had been given by her father Oswiu into Hild's care after the Battle of the river Winwæd. She was about twenty-six years old and held the abbey in conjunction with her mother, who had probably retired to Whitby about 670 on Oswiu's death in order to be near her daughter. It was a common practice in Ireland for monasteries to be under the rule of the founder's kin and to be passed on by hereditary right. Bede did not approve of this custom, as his letter to Archbishop Egbert of York clearly shows.[19] Benedict Biscop also cautions his monks at Wearmouth against electing an abbot "according to race."[20] Bede describes without comment how St. John of Beverley healed a sick nun named Cwenburh by his prayers. She was the daughter of the abbess of a monastery at Watton and it was her mother's intention that her daughter should succeed her as abbess.[21]

Ælfflæd's mother, Eanflæd, was the first Northumbrian to be baptized. After the death of Edwin she was taken to Kent, where she spent her childhood until she came up, a girl in her teens, to marry Oswiu, King of Northumbia, bringing a priest named Romanus to watch over her spiritual welfare. She was clearly a woman of much character and did not fail to observe the Roman Easter at a time which often differed from that of her husband by as much

---

[18] Taylor, I, 268 f.
[19] *EHD* I, 741.
[20] *HAB*, c. 11; Plummer, I, 375.
[21] *HE*, V, 3.

as two weeks. She also made Oswiu grant land at Gilling to establish a monastery in expiation for his responsibility for the death of Oswine in 651. She encouraged Wilfrid to make his first journey to Rome and probably helped Benedict Biscop too. And doubtless she was behind Alhfrith her stepson in his efforts with Wilfrid to bring about the Council of Whitby. So, unlike Hild, she was a supporter of Wilfrid and the Roman party. It is an interesting sidelight on this support that in 1879 there was found in Whitby a leaden bull or seal of seventh-century date with the inscription *Bonifatii archidiac*. This Boniface is in all probability the Roman cleric who befriended Wilfrid on his first visit.[22]

Ælfflæd, on the other hand, had been under the influence of Hild from her earliest childhood, so that she probably had less feeling for the Roman tradition than her mother. She was also a woman of wisdom and prudence and was known throughout the country and even abroad. There is a letter extant[23] written about 700, addressed to Adolana, Abbess of Pfalzel near Treves, commending one of Ælfflæd's friends, also an abbess, who, after having been detained by Ælfflæd, was now anxious to start on a journey, "long desired and often begun." Her Latin style is somewhat florid and not altogether unlike the style of Aldhelm. Fortunately she did not influence our author in that respect.

Ælfflæd was in many ways admirably fitted to unite the two groups of the Irish and Roman parties, so far as these groups still existed. On the one hand she was a great friend of St. Cuthbert and was able to give the Lindisfarne breth-

---

[22] W. Levison, *England and the Continent in the Eighth Century*, p. 17, n. 2.
[23] Tangl, No. 8, p. 3.

ren some information about him. She was cured of a very serious illness by a girdle that he sent her as a present.[24] She even persuaded him to leave his hermitage in 684 and meet her on Coquet Island, halfway between his Farne Island dwelling and Whitby. It was then that he prophesied the imminent death of her brother Ecgfrith and the accession of her stepbrother Aldfrith to the Northumbrian throne.[25] It must have been fairly soon afterwards that they again met, this time in a place called *Osingadun,* where there was apparently a newly established cell of Whitby with a church that Cuthbert was dedicating.[26] Though we do not know where *Osingadun* was, yet the ancient church at Kirkdale might possibly be the place, for it has early Saxon work in it, and there are some foundations of early buildings in the churchyard. What is even more suggestive of a Whitby connexion, the church is dedicated to St. Gregory. The ancient inscription still to be seen on the church sundial proves that this was the original dedication.[27]

On the other hand, Ælfflæd was also friendly with Wilfrid, and in 706 she was actively working at the council held by the river Nidd for the return of Wilfrid to Northumbria. Eddius describes her as "always the comforter and the best counsellor of the whole kingdom,"[28] and it was her pleading that finally led to the restoration of Wilfrid. Bede also speaks highly of her in his prose *Life of St. Cuthbert* and, making his favourite comparison be-

---

[24] *VP*, c. 23: *Two Lives*, p. 231.
[25] *VA*, III, 6: *Two Lives*, p. 102; *VP*, c. 24: *Two Lives*, p. 234.
[26] *VA*, IV, 10: *Two Lives*, p. 126; *VP*, 34, *Two Lives*, p. 260.
[27] Taylor, I, 357.
[28] *Eddius*, c. 60.

tween nobility of birth and nobility of mind, described her as having "increased the nobility of a royal pedigree by the much more potent nobility of the greatest virtues."[29]

Eanflæd and Ælfflæd were still acting as joint abbesses in 685, when the disastrous fight took place at Nechtansmere, in which Ecgfrith was killed and the Northumbrian ascendancy lost. As a result, Bishop Trumwine and his monks, no longer able to remain in Abercorn, migrated to Whitby. But perhaps the outstanding event during the later years of the seventh century was the translation of Edwin's relics to Whitby. Bede merely states that Edwin was buried there,[30] though in another place he says that Edwin's head was brought to York and placed in St. Gregory's chapel in the Church of St. Peter, which Edwin had begun to build and Oswald had finished.[31] The story of the translation to Whitby is told in detail by our author, and one gets the impression that a great deal of importance was attached to it. It is natural enough that Eanflæd should wish to have her father's bones lying in the church where her husband was buried and where she and her daughter were to be buried too. But there was probably more in it than that. The leading monastery in Lindsey was at Bardney, and Æthelred, King of Mercia, and his wife Osthryth, Eanflæd's daughter, were its great benefactors and perhaps founders. It may well have been looked upon as a rival establishment, particularly as it stood on territory which had changed hands between Northumbria and Mercia no less than seven times in the seventh century. Some time after its final recovery by Æthelred of Mercia from

---

[29] *VP*, c. 23: *Two Lives*, p. 231.
[30] *HE*, III, 24.
[31] *HE*, II, 20.

Ecgfrith at the Battle of the Trent in 679, Osthryth found the relics of her uncle St. Oswald and brought them to Bardney. The story as told by Bede[32] suggests that the monks were not anxious to receive the relics of their late conqueror; but Osthryth, aided by a miracle, won the day, and the bones of Oswald, or at least some of them, were placed here, though the head was in the coffin of St. Cuthbert, where it is believed to remain;[33] the arms also have a separate history. But in Offa's time the relics were still at Bardney, and Alcuin in his "Verses on the Saints of the Church of York" describes how Offa of Mercia adorned the tomb magnificently.[34] Eanflæd and Ælfflæd perhaps hoped that Edwin's relics might provide Whitby with a shrine and a cult as Oswald's were already doing. Oswald had perished fighting against his foes as Edwin had and the chief enemy of each was the heathen Penda, so that each was in a sense a martyr who died fighting for the faith. So Edwin's body was brought to Whitby, presumably headless, and the saga of the finding of the body provided a miraculous background not unlike the story of the finding of Oswald's relics, wonderful cures being associated with the place where Oswald fell in battle. By the end of the century many churches had their saints' bodies to which pilgrimages could be made. Lindisfarne had the uncorrupt body of St. Cuthbert, Ely the body of St. Æthelthryth, also uncorrupt, while Chad's body lay at Lichfield and Wilfrid's at Ripon; at all these, miracles of healing occurred and they became established

---

[32] *HE*, III, 11.

[33] For a further account of the extraordinary history of St. Oswald's relics see Plummer, II, 157 f.

[34] *MGH Poet. Lat.*, I, 160, lines 388 ff.

places of pilgrimage. It is not surprising that Osthryth at Bardney and Ælfflæd and Eanflæd at Whitby should have sought to establish shrines at which miracles might be expected to happen; nor would it be surprising if some rivalry had existed between them.

The Gregory cult of which we have spoken was established here at Whitby and, as at York and Canterbury, there was a porticus or chapel with an altar dedicated to the saint. The arts, too, were evident in the decoration of the church and of the sculptured stones and crosses which have been discovered in recent excavations on the site.[35] There is also still to be seen a remarkable cross in the church at Hackness, where one of the abbey cells was situated. The cross probably dates from the eighth century and is an excellent example of the kind of sculpture which was very popular especially in the North at this time.[36] So far as is known there are no examples of the illuminated Gospels or other painting and illumination such as have come down to us from Lindisfarne, Jarrow, and Wearmouth; nor do we definitely know of any scriptorium there, though it would be very surprising if none existed.

After the middle of the eighth century no certain information is available as to the history of the abbey. William of Malmesbury in his *Gesta Regum*,[37] written in the twelfth century, says that it was destroyed in the time of the Danish invasions (probably about 867). It would be about this time that it acquired its name of Whitby in place of the Old English name of Streoneshealh by which our

---

[35] See p. 34n6.
[36] G. B. Brown, *The Arts in Early England*, VI, i, 52-75, and Plates XIV-XIX; also Forest Scott, "The Hildithryth Stone and the Other Hartlepool Name-Stones," *Archaeologia Aeliana*, Fourth Series, XXXIV (1956), 196-212.
[37] *William of Malmesbury*, ed. W. Stubbs (*RS*, XC, 1867), I, 56.

author knows it. Symeon of Durham, another twelfth-century writer, tells of a remarkable revival of monasticism in the northeast.[38] A certain monk of Winchcomb monastery, named Ealdwine, having read in Bede's *History* of the wonderful monasteries which had once flourished in the kingdom of Northumbria, set out to find it in company with two Evesham monks and a donkey to carry their books and vestments. One was a priest named Ælfwig and the other an ex-soldier of William the Conqueror's army named Reinfrid who had been deeply impressed by the desolation of the Northeast while campaigning with the Conqueror. First they stopped at Newcastle but soon passed on to Wearmouth and Jarrow, which they rebuilt as best they could. Then Reinfrid went on to Whitby, where with some companions he settled down amid the ruins. In due course a monastery was once again established. When Reinfrid died he was buried at Hackness, and the Whitby monastery continued to flourish all through the Middle Ages until the dissolution of the monasteries by Henry VIII about the year 1538.

IV. Author and Date

WE HAVE no definite information about the author of the *Life,* but we can gather certain details about him from the work itself. First, he is an Englishman; in c. 6 he describes how on the Judgment Day Gregory will "bring us, that is the English race"; in c. 12 he mentions the time when "the English race came to this island." Further, he is a Northumbrian, for in c. 12 he speaks of "our nation, which is called the kingdom of the Humbrians"; in c. 16 Edwin is "our king" and in c. 17 Paulinus is "our teacher."

---

[38] Symeon of Durham, *Historia Dunelmensis Ecclesiae,* III, 21, ed. T. Arnold, I, 108 ff.

In c. 9 the "certain people of our nation" who arouse Gregory's interest in Rome prove to be people from Deira and the subjects of King Ælle. Lastly, in the story of the miraculous recovery of Edwin's relics in c. 18, the bones are to be taken to Whitby and in the course of c. 19 they are said to have been brought to "our monastery here." So we conclude that the author of the *Life* was a Whitby monk.[1]

The first part of the *Life* opens with the birth and early career of his hero and then, after the ninth chapter, when the work is just under way, the author concerns himself with English affairs from Gregory's first meeting with the English youths and his determination to convert their race down to the death of Paulinus and the translation of Edwin's bones in c. 19; thus almost half the *Life* is concerned with English affairs, with the emphasis naturally on Northumbria. Only the latter part is entirely concerned with Gregory and the miracles of which the tradition survived in the North of England.[2] But however much the writer may wander from his main subject, it is clear throughout that his earnest desire is to strengthen the cult of St. Gregory and to reflect the deep respect shown in England to the memory of the great Apostle of the English.

It is not possible to decide with certainty exactly when the *Life* was written. A copy was available to John the Deacon when he wrote his *Life* of the saint about 875, and the sole surviving manuscript is, as we have seen, to be dated early in the ninth century. But unquestionably it goes back to the century before. The translation of Edwin's

---

[1] See, further, Ewald, pp. 27 f.
[2] See below, pp. 50-51.

Author and Date

relics obviously plays an important part in the *Life*. These, we are told (c. 19), were placed near the altar of St. Gregory in the Church of St. Peter at Whitby. This not only helps to account for the curious fact that a quarter of the *Life* is devoted to Edwin and his relics but also suggests that the work was written not long after the translation.

What, then, was the date of the translation? We read in c. 18 that the story of the discovery of the relics was told the writer by one of his fellow-monks, a kinsman of the monk Trimma who found them. Eanflæd was alive when the incident took place, which puts it between 680, when Hild died, and the date of the death of Eanflæd. The date of Eanflæd's death is again a matter of uncertainty, though Bede tells us the date of her birth, the year 626.[3] A further limit is put by the statement (c. 18) that the translation was in the days of King Æthelred, who retired to a monastery in 704.[4] This statement also implies that Æthelred was no longer reigning when the *Life* was written and so we get an early limit to the composition of the *Life*. The writer in the course of the story in the same chapter adds that the man who appeared to Trimma in a dream told him that he was to remove Edwin's bones to *Streunes-alae* (Whitby), "which is the well-known monastery of Ælfflæd, a most religious woman and the daughter of Queen Eanflæd, who was herself, as we have said above, the daughter of Edwin." At once the question arises whether in this sentence the writer is still quoting the words of the man in the dream or adding an explanatory remark himself. The words "as we have said above" obviously refer to his own remark of a few sentences before. Surely, then, we

---

[3] *HE*, II, 9.
[4] *HE*, V, 24.

are justified in taking the sentence as the writer's own comment. Furthermore if the sentence had been part of the dream he would have made it clear that mother and daughter were ruling together at this time, as Bede tells us.[5] It therefore seems legitimate to assume that the writer is implying that Ælfflæd was still alive when he wrote, in which case the *Life* must have been written between 704 and 714.

Another slight indication of date is found in c. 16 where the writer is telling the story of Paulinus's appearance to Edwin at the court of King Rædwald, some little time before Edwin became king in 617. The incident is said by the writer to have happened "long before the time of any who are now alive." This statement would fit in with a date even as early as 700 (see p. 149, note 64) but perhaps not much earlier, though one has to remember that the author may have been a little vague about the date of the incident.

There are other reasons too for supposing that the work was written in the first or second decade of the eighth century. One of these is the form in which the *Life* is written. Quite early in the eighth century or even before, the Anglo-Saxon Church, especially in the North, became familiar with certain saints' Lives which were to exercise a strong influence over the hagiographic literature of Western Europe. First and foremost among these was the Latin translation of St. Athanasius's *Life of Antony* made by a certain Evagrius who became Bishop of Antioch in 388. Another was Jerome's *Life of Paul the Hermit,* while a third, written by Sulpicius Severus in the fifth century, was the *Life of St. Martin.* These set a kind of pattern for the

---

[5] *HE,* IV, 26.

typical saint's Life of the period. But we can say categorically that our writer was not affected by these, even though they were being used by a writer in Lindisfarne about the turn of the century when he was writing a Life of St. Cuthbert.[6] About 721 Bede himself wrote a Life of St. Cuthbert on the same model,[7] based largely on the work of the earlier anonymous monk of Lindisfarne. When, between 725 and 731, Bede composed his Martyrology, it is clear that he had at his disposal no less than fifty hagiographical texts. But our author knew none of these Lives; so far as he follows any previous work, he may be said to have based his on Gregory's *Dialogues,* with which we know he was familiar. But he does not use the dialogue form. He is, in fact, clearly experimenting.[8] The result sets it apart from other eighth-century saints' Lives, and for this reason C. W. Jones is inclined to date it a generation before the Lives mentioned above,[9] which would throw it back into the seventh century. But this does not fit in with the remark in c. 16 quoted above, about the appearance of Paulinus. So, on the whole, it seems most likely that the work was written between 704 and 714 and probably nearer to the latter date. For the present we must be content to accept the fact that the dating is by no means definite until further evidence is found. But almost certainly we can claim that it shares with the anonymous Life of St. Cuthbert mentioned above the right to be called one of the two earliest extant pieces of written literature produced by the Anglo-Saxons.

---

[6] *Two Lives,* p. 12.
[7] *Two Lives,* p. 16.
[8] See below, p. 52.
[9] C. W. Jones, *Saints' Lives and Chronicles,* p. 65.

V. Sources

THE WRITER of the *Life* has much to say concerning his lack of information about Gregory. Thus in c. 3 he complains that "in the record of his deeds" he has heard of "but a few miracles." What the writer may well mean is that there is no extant *Liber de virtutibus* such as was to be found in the case of other saints. But in c. 5 he promises to "relate those facts" about Gregory "which the fame of his holiness has preserved among us, derived from various sources and from ancient times." This obviously refers to the tradition preserved at Whitby. The account of Gregory's meeting with the Deiran youths in Rome is based on a story "told by the faithful" (c. 9), while the account of Edwin's conversion (c. 16) is told "not in the condensed form in which we heard it," by which he probably refers to a brief entry in some chronicle to which he had access in the monastery; it cannot be the words of those who knew him "better than most" because it happened "long before the days of any of those who are still alive"; so it has to be the record of "faithful witnesses"—in other words, the traditions available in the monastery. These were perhaps told on some winter evening in place of the ancient Germanic tragic stories, against the recital of which Alcuin warned the monks of Lindisfarne.[1]

There are traditions, too, about Paulinus—as, for instance, the story of his mysterious appearance to Edwin at the court of King Rædwald (c. 16), an account which differs somewhat from the version of the story which Bede tells:[2] there are also stories which Bede does not know, such as the saint's clever rebuttal of an incident with a

---
[1] *MGH Epp.*, IV, No. 124, p. 183.
[2] *HE*, II, 12.

crow which threatened to disturb the superstitious minds of the Northumbrian catechumens (c. 15); and the death of Paulinus (c. 17) and how his soul was carried to heaven in the shape of a swan, "related by some who saw it." The account of the translation of Edwin's relics (cc. 18 and 19) is naturally based throughout on the local tradition.

So he ends the section dealing with the English and in c. 20 he begins to go further afield in order to get back to his original subject, the life and miracles of Gregory. Here again, in the series of miracles related in cc. 20-23, 26, 28, and 29, he is dependent on "ancient stories," only one of which (c. 29) is said definitely to be derived from Roman tradition, though the scene of each story is set in Rome. He apologizes when telling the story of the conversion of the Lombard king, because he does not know full details; in fact he is not even sure whether it was a Lombard king (c. 23). Referring to the whole group of stories at the end of the same chapter, he says, quoting Gregory himself, that he is not always able to give the exact words of the speakers, because, if he did, he might miss the spiritual lessons involved. The story of the white dove's dictating the Ezekiel Homilies (c. 26) survived in Rome in a slightly different form and is related by John the Deacon.[3] It seems to have influenced early pictures of the saint.[4] John does not repeat the Whitby tradition of the death of Gregory's successor to the papacy; the naïve and cruel story with its echoes of Germanic folklore as told by our author (c. 28) could hardly have survived in Rome in its English form.

---

[3] John the Deacon's *Life*, IV, 70: *PL*, LXXV, 222.
[4] See p. 157n110. Also "Observationes Angeli Roccae de imaginibus S. Gregorii magni," *PL*, LXXV, 463 ff.

A story said to have been derived from Roman tradition tells of the miraculous salvation of the Emperor Trajan who was rescued from hell by Gregory's tears (c. 29). Even our author has some qualms about it, and John the Deacon, who attributes it, in his turn, to Anglo-Saxon sources, is clearly troubled by its questionable orthodoxy.[5] It is the only one of this group of stories whose origins he admits, though it is quite clear that they are all derived from the Whitby *Life*.

In c. 30 the writer gives a long apology for his work. He has done the best he can. He apologizes to any who know more about the miracles than he does; he then goes on to apologize for the confused arrangement of the miracles. This might perhaps refer to the fact that he has mixed up stories of Edwin with those of Gregory; but it is much more likely that he is familiar with and has used a well-known saga without necessarily following the regular order of the saga as generally told. He even goes so far as to apologize for altering the words though keeping the sense. He is, as he says in c. 3, trying to write a book about Gregory and he prays his "readers" to overlook his faults; the long apology in c. 30 is also addressed to the reader. It might almost be said that he is experiencing and apologizing for the difficulties of the transition between the saga-maker and the writer. After all, he says, the writers of the Gospels have had to alter the wording and order of the same incident from Gospel to Gospel. He is even prepared to believe that part of the saga belongs to some other saint; so he puts forward the ingenious excuse that, as we all belong to one body, so all the members may be said to have all things in common, and what is true of the whole body is true of the individual members.

---

[5] John the Deacon's *Life*, II, 45: *PL*, LXXV, 105; and p. 161n*122*.

Sources

But whence did this saga tradition originally derive? It is probable that ultimately it came from Canterbury. Eanflæd was baptized by Paulinus and taken by him to Kent after the death of Edwin at the Battle of Hatfield in 633.[6] There she remained until some time after 642, when she returned to Northumbria to marry King Oswiu.[7] Clearly, both Eanflæd and her chaplain Romanus must have heard many stories of Gregory from Paulinus, who knew Gregory personally. Bede also uses traditional stories about Gregory, but these are less extensive than the Whitby saga. But he had one great advantage which the Whitby writer did not have, in that at some time while writing his *History* he came into possession of letters both from Gregory and other Popes that helped to raise his work from legend into history. The Gregory material used by our author was later eagerly taken over by Continental biographers, but the new Paulinus and Edwin material was never incorporated into later English history. This would seem to imply that the Whitby *Life* was better known on the Continent than in England, quite possibly because a copy, perhaps the only copy, was taken by some pilgrim or missionary from Whitby to the Continent during the eighth century. But when Bede's great *History* became well known at home and abroad, it soon replaced the limited and halting work of the Whitby monk.

Our author was familiar with most of the main works of Gregory. His knowledge of the Scripture is also very wide. He quotes frequently from the Psalms, as would be expected, and from at least seven other Old Testament

---

[6] James the Deacon, who remained in Northumbria when Paulinus fled in 633 (*HE*, II, 20), may also have preserved traditions of Gregory and the Roman missionaries, in the north of England.

[7] *HE*, III, 15.

books. Of the Gospels his favourite book is undoubtedly St. Matthew's, while his favourite epistle is the First Epistle of St. Paul to the Corinthians. There are few books of the New Testament from which he does not quote in scriptural quotations and allusions, which number altogether about a hundred. He normally uses the Vulgate, but Old Latin versions were known at Whitby, too (cf. c. 30 and p. 164n*132*).

Our author, as we have seen, alludes to Jerome and Augustine, but apart from one somewhat unexpected quotation adapted from Horace (c. 25) there is no sign of any classical learning. Quite possibly it was looked upon with disfavour at Whitby, so that copies of classical authors would not readily be available. Indeed the Horace quotation is one which might be found in any Latin grammar of the type that Bede used; a surprising number of this kind were available at the end of the seventh century in England.[8] So it does not imply any first-hand knowledge of the works of Horace; nor indeed is there any indication of such reading. What is perhaps more surprising is that our author shows no signs of any knowledge of Virgil, though Bede quotes him frequently.[9]

The only other book which he uses is the *Liber Pontificalis*,[10] from which he obtains details of the parentage of Gregory, though he adds the name of the saint's mother, Sylvia, which he obtains from some other source. And indeed it is clear that it was on tradition, not literary sources, that the writer principally depended.

---

[8] M. L. W. Laistner, "The Library of the Venerable Bede," *BLTW*, p. 241.
[9] Plummer, I, lii, n. 3.
[10] W. Levison, "Bede as Historian," *BLTW*, p. 120.

VI. The Author's Latin Style

The Latin style of our author is poor in comparison with that of Bede, as all who have written on the *Life* are agreed.[1] It is only fair to say that we have only one MS and that pretty clearly the work of a careless scribe. Unfortunately the only edition of the complete *Life* so far produced is full of inaccuracies and this has added to the general confusion. But the fact remains that the author's style is crabbed, awkward, and ungrammatical even by contemporary standards. It is often ambiguous and so the translator in a few places finds himself faced with almost insoluble problems. It would seem that little rhetoric was taught at Whitby in the writer's time. His sentence construction is involved, his word-order confusing, his vocabulary limited. Unlike Bede he seldom stops to pluck the flowers of oratory; but fortunately he is not influenced by the strange bombastic style of the *Hisperica Famina* type with its alliteration, periphrasis, and exotic vocabulary, such as make the works of Aldhelm repellent and almost unreadable. Reminiscences of St. Gregory, as is not surprising, appear in turns of style, in syntactical usage, and in vocabulary.[2] But making all allowances for the looser syntax of early Medieval Latin, one can hardly believe that such a Latin style would have been tolerated at Jarrow in the days of Bede. We should have seen fewer redundant

---

[1] "Der üble Latein der Vita," *Ewald*, p. 17; "schrecklich verwilderte Latein," *Brechter*, p. 119; "the illiterate author who blunderingly composed," *Thurston*, p. 339.

[2] Some words commonly used by Gregory and fairly frequent in our author are: *concite, merito, non (nec) immerito, scilicet, terribiliter* and other adverbs ending in *-ter, rimare, lassescere, effulgere*. He occasionally uses the noun *Veritas* to denote Christ, a term which is found frequently in Gregory's writings.

infinitives,[3] for instance, less bewildering use of personal pronouns,[4] less frequent violation of the sequence of tenses,[5] or less of the tiresome habit of obscuring the sense by changing the order of words.[6] But in spite of all these drawbacks, he can usually tell a good straightforward story; one may instance his description of the violent reaction of the Roman citizens when Pope Benedict gave Gregory permission to depart (c. 10), the locust that brought him back *(ibid.)*, the vision of Trimma (c. 19), and especially the series of Gregory's miracles (cc. 20-22, 29) which are also told by John the Deacon (II, 41-44) but less vividly. It is when our author seeks to comment or to put forward theological and philosophical theories that he becomes involved and turgid.

VII. The Relation Between Bede and the Whitby Writer

Much has been said about the relationship between Bede's *History* and the Whitby *Life,* ever since Ewald raised the question in his famous articles (see below, pp. 60-62). He attempted very unconvincingly to show likenesses between the two versions of the story of the Deiran youths.[1] But, as we shall see, the two versions are more striking in their

---

[3] Thus *dixisse* in the first sentence of c. 3; *debuisse,* first sentence of c. 10; promittente *voluisse,* c. 16; invenit *habere,* c. 21.

[4] Many examples could be given of the confused use of pronouns but one example will suffice. This is the sentence in c. 28 beginning, *"Quo magnum,"* where *eumque* refers to the monk, *eius* to hell, *eum* to Gregory, *eius* to Christ, *eo* to hell, *se* to the monk, and the second *se* to Gregory.

[5] Cf. c. 7, *querebat;* c. 10, *dedisse, potuit;* c. 15, *nescisset, dominantur, praenuntiet.*

[6] For example, in such confused sentences as the last sentence in c. 6, or c. 16, sentence beginning *"Hoc igitur";* c. 24, first sentence; and many others.

[1] *HE,* II, 1, and c. 9 below.

Bede and the Whitby Writer

differences than their likenesses. The description of the early life of Gregory in both books depends on borrowings from the same sources, so that Plummer's attempts to show a relationship[2] are mostly irrelevant. In the unlikely event that the Whitby *Life* is later than Bede's *History*, our writer would almost certainly have seen a copy. Then he would hardly have complained of lack of information. There would have been plenty for him to use, notably from Gregory's letters, which Bede used but with which the Whitby monk was clearly unfamiliar. There are several mistakes which the latter would then have been able to avoid;[3] there is the famous *Libellus Responsionum*, which Bede quotes in full but which he does not mention; lastly, there is a copy of the epitaph on the saint's grave which the Whitby monk would certainly have wanted to incorporate. Of course it may be argued that our author was chiefly interested in Gregory's miracles, but, even so, it seems difficult to believe that he would have entirely neglected everything else that Bede could offer.

On the other hand, it is not difficult to show that it is very unlikely that Bede had ever seen the Whitby *Life*. Bede, who loved a picturesque story, would scarcely have omitted the account of Gregory's attempted missionary journey to England and the message of the locust. Moreover, what story, with its vivid account of Gregory's desperate efforts to achieve his purpose, could better have illustrated the saint's devotion to the English people? He would not have failed to tell how Paulinus's soul was carried to heaven in the form of a swan; and it is most unlikely that he would have failed to incorporate the account

---

[2] Plummer, II, 389-91.
[3] See pp. 146-47n50.

of the translation of Edwin's relics, with its attendant miracles, especially as Edwin was a king whom Bede greatly admired. He had in fact already related a somewhat similar story of the discovery and translation of the relics of King Oswald, another typical Christian ruler and warrior saint.

Several writers have called attention to the fact that the set of miracles related by the Whitby monk in cc. 20-29, the stories of the unbelieving matron, the relic rags, the demon-possessed horse, the healing of the tyrant king, the dove's dictating to Gregory, and the story of the salvation of Trajan's soul from hell are all found in the interpolated version of Paul the Deacon's Life. He even tells the grim story of Gregory's assault on his successor, Sabianus. John the Deacon also borrows four of the stories.[4] From these two sources these miracle stories spread all over Europe. It would indeed have been strange if Bede had not used some or all of these if he had known them. Any student familiar with Bede's miracle stories will know that it is no answer to say that Bede would not have cared to use such wildly improbable tales. Some of the stories in the *History* associated with the names of Alban and Oswald and of Fursa and the Barking nuns are equally fantastic.

Other indications make it seem unlikely that Bede consulted the Whitby *Life*. It is clear that both writers use a copy of some part of the *Liber Pontificalis* for details of the parentage of Gregory but that only our author knows his mother's name, Sylvia, a clear sign that he had access to Roman tradition which Bede did not have. John the Deacon, unlike the Langobardic Paul the Deacon, also knows

---

[4] John the Deacon's *Life of St. Gregory*. II, 41, 42, 43, 44: *PL,* LXXV, 103-06.

the name obviously from the Roman tradition. He even describes in some detail a portrait of her—all from local knowledge, of course. Other reasons too could be adduced, not the least being that Bede generally acknowledges his sources when he is using an earlier Life. Thus in his account of Fursa and of the miracles associated with the monastery at Barking he acknowledges that he is using such an earlier Life,[5] while in the Preface to the *History* he acknowledges his debt to the anonymous Lindisfarne *Life of St. Cuthbert*.[6] It is true that in his account of Wilfrid's life Bede does not mention his indebtedness to Eddius, but he may have had some reason for not doing so, connected with his somewhat ambiguous relations with Wilfrid. Altogether the evidence seems to be strong enough that each writer was independent of the other; and indeed Bede seems to have had little connexion with Whitby or knowledge of its doings after the death of Hild in 680.

VIII. LATER HISTORY OF THE LIFE

THE EARLIEST KNOWN REFERENCE to an Anglo-Saxon Life of St. Gregory is found in the Life of the saint written by John the Deacon somewhere about 875. In his Preface John describes how, at the vigil of the Feast of the saint celebrated in Rome at the Church of St. John Lateran, Pope John VIII, who was officiating, enquired why there was no Life of the saint available even in his own church when a Life of him was to be found "among the Saxons and the Langobardi."[1] The latter Life is the one written more than

---

[5] *HE*, III, 19: IV, 10.
[6] Bede does not specifically mention this Lindisfarne Life in his Prologue to the prose *Life of St. Cuthbert*, perhaps, as Levison suggests, for reasons of delicacy. See *BLTW*, p. 127, n. 1, and *Two Lives*, p. 341.
[1] *PL*, LXXV, 61.

a century before by Paul the Deacon, who was a Langobard.[2] The Saxon Life can be definitely shown to be our *Life*, for there are a number of verbal quotations from it. John quotes from Paul's Life too, but the form in which he knew it was the original form. Somewhere about the end of the ninth century an unknown interpolator added several sections of the Whitby *Life* to Paul's work, but clearly it is not this interpolated version that John is quoting. Therefore John must have had access to a copy of the Whitby *Life* when he was writing in Rome about 875.

We have to wait for the next reference until the early eighteenth century, when Canisius in his *Thesaurus* refers to a Life in another codex at St. Gall, which he declares to be so full of fables that if he had published it he would have laid himself open to criticism and even ridicule.[3] So it was not until 1866 that Dr. Paul Ewald, who was working on a study of St. Gregory's letters, ran across it and printed considerable extracts from it, in a volume of essays devoted to the memory of Georg Waitz.[4] He also added a most illuminating commentary on the *Life* in which he established the fact that the author was a monk who lived at Whitby. He further discussed the relationship between the Whitby *Life* and the Lives by Paul the Deacon and John the Deacon. He maintained that the work was earlier than Bede and put it down tentatively to the first decade of the eighth century. He also maintained that Bede probably knew and used the *Life* to some extent.

A lively interest was quickly aroused among scholars by the appearance of this newly discovered *Life*. The earli-

---

[2] *PL*, LXXV, 42-60.

[3] H. Canisius, *Thesaurus monumentorum ecclesiasticorum et historicorum*, tomi II, pars III (Amsterdam, 1725), p. 252.

[4] P. Ewald, "Die älteste Biographie Gregors I." See Bibliography.

est notice was a review of Ewald's article by Edmund Bishop in the *Downside Review*[5] in which the writer summarized Ewald's article and quoted passages from it. He also pointed out some interesting liturgical features in the *Life*, such as the words of administration reported by the writer as having been used by Gregory in the story of the unbelieving matron; and of course the proof that the doctrine of transubstantiation was held by the English Church in the seventh century.

In 1888 Sir John Seeley, writing an obituary notice on Ewald for the *English Historical Review*,[6] summarized the article on the *Life* and quoted extracts from the *Life*, much as Ewald had done. In 1896 Charles Plummer also printed extracts from it in an appendix to his edition of the *Ecclesiastical History* of Bede.[7] It was a pity that Plummer had not heard of the original article until his book was in print. If he had had a little longer to think, he would probably have changed his mind about the implications of the verbal likenesses between Bede and the Whitby monk.

Had Ewald lived longer there is every likelihood that he would have given us an outstanding and perhaps definitive edition of the *Life;* but it was not until 1904 that Cardinal Gasquet published the complete text.[8] He followed the chapter divisions suggested by Ewald (for the MS has no chapter divisions), though in at least one place (cc. 21-22) he divided them up wrongly. He had the advantage of being allowed the loan of the volume from the St. Gall Library, but in spite of this the result was far from satisfactory. The introduction adds little to what Ewald

---

[5] Edmund Bishop, *Downside Review*, V (1886), 271-74.
[6] J. R. Seeley, "Paul Ewald and Pope Gregory I," *EHR*, III (1888), 295-310.
[7] Plummer, II, 389-91.
[8] F. A. Gasquet, *A Life of Pope Gregory the Great* (London, 1904).

had already said or more strictly what Bishop had summarized of Ewald's introduction in the review mentioned above. The number of mistakes made in transcribing the text added confusion to an already very difficult and confused text.

Father Herbert Thurston in reviewing the edition[9] did not fail to call attention to the inaccuracy of Gasquet's text, pointing out mistakes that he had discovered by comparing the printed text with the two photographic facsimiles reproduced in the edition. He continued the discussion of the relationship between Bede's *History* and the Whitby *Life* and suggested that our author had the *History* before him when he wrote. Finally he concluded that there is no proof that the *Life* was written before 780.

One of the most remarkable contributions to the discussion of the date and sources of the *Life* was that made by Abbot E. C. Butler,[10] who came to the conclusion that neither Bede nor the monk of Whitby was aware of the work of the other and that there is no need to alter drastically the date of composition assigned by Ewald—namely, the first decade of the eighth century.

The *Life* has been known to scholars since 1906, but surprisingly little attention has been paid to it. This may be partly due to the exaggerated notion of the corruptness of the text and the difficulties of interpretation, for which Gasquet's edition must bear some of the blame. But in 1939 Dr. C. E. Wright in his discussion of the remains of saga

---

[9] H. Thurston, "The Oldest Life of Gregory," *Month*, CIV(1904), 337-53.

[10] E. C. Butler, "Chronicle, Hagiographica," *Journal of Theological Studies*, VII (1906), 312-13.

The Manuscript

material in England[11] had much that is of interest to say about the question of the origin of some of the traditional stories told by the Whitby monk and by Bede; his whole discussion is particularly important in that it relates the saga material of the *Life* to the general oral and traditional heritage of the seventh and eighth centuries in England.

C. W. Jones also has much to say about the *Life* in his study of early saints' Lives.[12] His general observations on the text lead him to the conclusion that the *Life* was written a full generation earlier than the other early Lives which have come down to us from English sources. He also adds in the Appendix the first complete English translation, though T. L. Almond had already translated some parts of it.[13] It is only fair to Jones to point out that he was compelled to use Gasquet's erratic text, but even so, his book contains a number of mistranslations. A much more accurate translation of a few chapters of the Life by Professor Whitelock is to be found in *EHD I*, 687-90.

IX. THE MANUSCRIPT

THE MANUSCRIPT of the Life of Gregory printed below, the only surviving copy, was written on the Continent, probably during the early part of the ninth century. It is now part of Codex 567 in the monastic library of St. Gall, Switzerland.[1] The volume consists of seven different items,

---

[11] C. E. Wright, *The Cultivation of Saga in Anglo-Saxon England*, pp. 43-48, 85-91.

[12] C. W. Jones, *Saints' Lives and Chronicles*, pp. 64-67, 97-121.

[13] T. L. Almond, "The Whitby Life of Gregory," *Downside Review*, XXIII (1904), N.S., IV, 15-29.

[1] For a further account of the MS see Brechter, p. 118; G. Scherrer, *Verzeichniss der Handschriften des Stiftsbibliothek von S. Gallen* (Halle, 1875), p. 182; H. F. Brauer, *Die Bücherei von S. Gallen und das althochdeutsche Schrifttum* (Halle, 1926), pp. 12, 17, 41, 55; A. Bruckner, *Scriptoria medii*

all Lives of saints and associated material; the original items were all written separately and bound together somewhere in the ninth century, for the codex is listed in a ninth-century catalogue as follows: *Vita sancti silvestri et sancti gregorii, hilarii episcopi et eiusdem epistola ad filiam suam abram et lucii confessoris atque lonochildis episcopi et goaris in volumine. I.*[2] The contents as listed in this catalogue agree exactly with those of our codex, with the single exception that the final item is no longer the *Vita Goaris*. In its place are now found the *Actus sancti Martini* and the associated items listed below, occupying in all four extra quires. Sometime in the fifteenth century the quires in the codex were numbered. The arabic figures which mark each of them from 1 to 12 are preserved, but quires 13-16 were so severely cut that only traces of the numbers remain; there is enough left, however, to show that the pieces about Saint Martin had already replaced the *Vita Goaris* when the quire numbers were added. So it is possible that in 1461, when there was a general rebinding of the St. Gall manuscripts, the *Vita Goaris,* which was the last item and which by that time may have been worn and damaged, was replaced by the quires of Martin material. At any rate the replacement occurred not later than the fifteenth century.

---

aevi helvetica, II, *Schreibschulen der Diözese Konstanz S. Gallen*, I (Geneva, 1936), 79; E. Munding, *Das Verzeichnis der St. Galler Heiligenleben und ihrer Handschriften in Codex Sangall. No. 566* (Texte und Arbeiten herausgegeben durch die Erzabtei Beuron. Vol. I. Abteilung. Heft 3/4, Beuron, 1918), pp. 129-34; L. Traube, *Nomina Sacra* (Munich, 1907), p. 219; W. Levison, *MGH Script. rerum Merov*, VII, No. 726, p. 680; K. Loffler, "Die Sankt-Galler Schreibschule in der 2 Halfte des 8 Jahrhunderts," *Palaeographia Latina*, VI (1929), 40 ff.; E. A. Lowe, *Codices Latini Antiquiores*, VII, No. 943, p. 30.

[2] G. Becker, *Catalogi Bibliothecarum Antiqui* (Bonn, 1885), No. 279, p. 49; P. Lehmann, *Mittelalterliche Bibliothekskataloge Deutschlands und der Schweiz*, I (Munich, 1918), 78, line 2.

The Manuscript

The binding is late medieval and consists of a grey scraped leather band which reaches halfway across the front and back wooden boards; the rest is uncovered. Inside the front board is a guard paper with a list of contents made by Ildefons von Arx, the librarian from 1824 to 1833. The back board has no guard page. On the wood of the front board, in a fifteenth-century hand now almost illegible, is a list of contents that includes the Life of St. Goar. Possibly the scribe, copying from an old catalogue, was unaware of the alteration that was made in the last item, or perhaps the list on the board was made before the rebinding was done. The fastening consists of a leather strap attached to a small metal plate on the back board. The strap is fastened by a small metal tag to a pin in the middle of the front board. It is contemporary with the binding.

The modern pagination should run up to page 200, but because two consecutive pages have been numbered 113 by mistake, it reaches only to 199. The contents are as follows:

I. 1-73, *Gesta S. Silvestri*. All in a single ninth-century hand. *BHL*, 7725-27, 7732-33, 7735.
   p. 74, scribbles.
   $1^8, 2^8, 3^8, 4^8, 5^6$ lacking leaf 6, presumably a blank leaf cut away.
II. 75-110, *Vita S. Gregorii*. In two ninth-century hands. It has been corrected throughout by still another scribe. See below. *BHL*, 3637. $6^8, 7^{12}$ lacking leaves 1 and 2, presumably blank leaves cut away.
III. 111-33, *Vita S. Hilarii auctore Fortunato*. Also *Epistula ad filiam suam Abram*. *BHL*, 3885, 3887, 3887a, Suppl.
   133, end of *Vita*. *Initium hymni Hilarii*. All in the same ninth-century hand.
   134, blank.
IV. 135-53, *Conversio vel vita beatissimi Lucii*. All in a single ninth-century hand. *BHL*, 5024.
   10^6 lacking leaves 3 and 5; 11^8 lacking leaves 7 and 8.
   Quire 11 is a palimpsest. The lower writing shows that the

original manuscript was a half-uncial copy of the Vulgate version of portions of the Old Testament. It was written in the late fifth or early sixth century, so that the portions here preserved together with the seventy-five other pages from the same MS, used in the St. Gall MS 193, form the oldest extant text of the Vulgate version of these passages.[3] The portions preserved in quire 11 are:

pp. 142-43, Micah 2:7-3:3.
pp. 144-45, Micah 4:2-4:10.
pp. 146-47, Amos 8:10-9:5.
pp. 148-49, Malachi 1:11-2:6.
pp. 150-51, Malachi 1:1-1:10.
pp. 152-53, Jonah 1:6-2:2.
Page 153 was not used a second time.
Page 154, first page of quire 12, is blank.

V. 155-163, *Vita S. Lonochilii et S. Agnofledae*. All in a single late eighth-century hand. *BHL*, 4966.
12^6 lacking leaf 6.

VI. 164-70, *Actus S. Martini*. All in a single ninth-century hand. *BHL*, 5610. Page 171, one line of text and musical notes in a later hand. Otherwise blank.
13^4.

VII. 172-99, continuation of the above but in an earlier eighth-century hand.
Also the *Epistula ad Aurelium, BHL*, 5612,
the *Epistula ad Bassulam, BHL*, 5613,
and a description of the basilica of St. Martin, *BHL*, 5624c Suppl.
All in a single hand.
14^6, 15^6 lacking leaf 6, and 16^4 lacking leaf 4.

Though it is likely that the section of IV containing the Life of Lucius over the ancient Bible text came from Chur, there is no reason to suppose that any of the other items in the codex were not written at St. Gall. It will be clear from

---

[3] E. A. Lowe, "A Hand-list of Half-uncial Manuscripts," *Miscellanea Francesco Ehrle IV* (*Studi e Testi*, vol. 40), p. 55; A. Dold, *Prophetentexte* (Texte und Arbeiten, I Abteilung, Heft 1,2, 1917), pp. xiv ff.

The Manuscript

the above account that each item is on quires which are independent of each other. If an item does not cover the whole quire, the blank sheets are removed and the odd pages left blank.

The section with which we are particularly concerned, pages 75-110, is written mostly in two hands, of which the first covers pages 75-106—that is, to the end of the quire. Two leaves were then added to the last quire, on which the *Life* was completed by another scribe, who worked more carefully than the first scribe, though his handwriting is less pleasing. Both scribes belong to the ninth century, and both write in the script sometimes called the Swiss or Rhaetic hand. There is little doubt that both were trained in the same scriptorium. The first scribe writes twenty-five lines, the second twenty-six lines, to the page. Each page measures 12 x 17.5 cms. The ruling was made before folding. There are double bounding lines with the pricking of the guide lines showing clearly on the outside page of each quire (i.e., 75/76, 89/90, 91/92, 105/06, and also on the outer of the two sheets added later, 107/08). The parchment, which was finely smoothed, was arranged with the hair facing outwards. The ink used by the first scribe is dark brown. The title is in half-uncial script tinted red, and the two initial letters on the first page are also red.

Features of the hand are the frequent use of the ampersand for *et* in whatever position, even initially (e.g., *etiam*), and the fairly common joint *c*'s to represent an *a*. Ligatures are found with *r* and vowels following it as well as for *rm* and *rt;* occasionally the crossed *r* is used to represent *rum*. Other ligatures are *st*, frequent throughout, and also *et*, less frequent. There are a number of examples of the horned *o*, looking almost like an uncial *d*. Cedillas

are used occasionally to represent *æ,* and sometimes they are used even with the final *e* of an adverb or the final *e* of a present active infinitive as in, e.g., *congruę, aperirę,* (c. 26). In one or two instances an *æ* or *œ* is found in place of an *e,* as in *ræstauravit* (c. 30), *cingæbantur* (c. 7), *Iohannæ* (c. 26). The usual abbreviations of *per, post,* and *prae* and of the *nomina sacra* and *m* and *n* suspensions are found particularly at the end of a line. There are occasional *-ur* and *-us* suspensions. The first scribe uses comparatively few abbreviations in the first part of the *Life,* but, as he proceeds, the hand grows tighter and the abbreviations more frequent, possibly because he was beginning to realize that the two quires at his disposal were not likely to be sufficient. Punctuation consists of the point, the double point, the double point with the second point tailed, the tick, the colon, the semicolon, and the reversed semicolon (generally used as a question mark). The point and the tick are used indiscriminately.

Later than the first scribe, though probably not much later, perhaps when the different sections of the codex were collected, the second scribe added the four missing pages, presumably from the same exemplar. The hands differ very little. Both have two significant Rhaetic features, the use of *t* with a headstroke curving downwards on the left and the tendency to confuse *e* and *i* spellings. One or two of this later scribe's letter-forms are different, especially his *g*'s, which have a closed tail; his handwriting is smaller and he uses a slightly paler ink. Finally, still another scribe went through the whole *Life,* probably sometime in the ninth century, using a somewhat ugly rough hand, altering spellings, and correcting the frequent grammatical and spelling mistakes of the first scribe; he inserted

Notes on the Text

omissions from the scribe's exemplar, though this exemplar was clearly far from impeccable.

There is no evidence to show that the exemplar used was the original copy brought across from Whitby. If it had been, it would have been written in an insular hand that might have presented difficulties for the scribe, some of which could well have been reflected in the text. This of course is not necessarily so, because in the ninth-century catalogue there is a list of no less than twenty-nine works that are *"scottice scripti."* But, on the other hand, the spelling of proper nouns or names, such as *Streunes-Alae, Hedfled, Lindissi* (with the final *si* mistaken for the conjunction; all in c. 18), and *Uuestanglorum* for the East Angles (c. 16), suggests that the scribe can hardly have been copying directly from an exemplar written by one familiar with these English names.

Notes on the Text

Readings marked *M1* in the footnotes represent the original scribe's version.

Readings marked *M2* represent alterations made by the corrector who went all through the manuscript making various alterations. (Cf. above, pp. 68-69.)

Readings marked *M3* occur only on pages 107-10 of the manuscript and represent the work of another scribe.

When the editor adopts an *M2* reading, he cites the version of the first scribe in the notes, marking it *M1*. The version of the second scribe (pages 107-10 of the manuscript) will, in the same circumstances, be marked *M3*.

When the editor makes any alteration in the text, the abbreviation *ed.* notes the fact.

Punctuation and capitals are mostly as in the manuscript, but the editor has occasionally altered these to conform to modern practice.

Both scribes use a hooked *e* to represent *ae,* but, as will be observed, are far from consistent in using them. These hooks are represented in the printed text by cedillas.

The end of each manuscript page is marked by a slant. The numbers of the pages are given in the margin.

TEXT AND TRANSLATION

p. 75 INCIPIT LIBER BEATI ET LAUDABILIS VIRI GREGORII PAPĘ URBIS ROMĘ DE VITA ATQUE EIUS[1] VIRTUTIBUS

IN PRIMIS PROEMIUM

Cum suos sancta per orbem ecclesia catholica in omni gente doctores semper celebrare non cessat, quos Christo Domino magistrante ad se directos in eo gloriando congaudet, eisque scriptis memorialibus promulget in posteros, ut ponant in Deo spem suam et non obliviscantur operum Dei sui et mandata eius exquirant. Merito nos quoque nostri mentionem magistri possumus iuxta vires nostras adiuvante Domino facere, describentes quem sanctum Gregorium cum omni etiam orbe prefato possumus appellare.

FINIT PREFACIUNCULA.

[Chapter 1]

Fuit igitur iste natione Romanus, ex patre Gordiano et matre Silvia, nobilis secundum legem sed nobilior corde coram Deo in religione. Longo iam tempore manens in monasterio, ubi eius animo labentia cuncta subterfuisse ipse designat. Rebus omnibus quę volvuntur eminebat, nulla nisi celestia cogitare consuerat.

[Chapter 2]

Unde etiam aptius ad hec qualiter venisset, carptim breviterque eius perfruamur sermone et sensu. Primo namque

---

[1] *above M2*

Here begins the book of that blessed and praiseworthy man, Gregory, Pope of the city of Rome: his life and miracles.

First, the Prologue[1]

The holy catholic Church throughout the world never ceases to celebrate the learned men of every race and rejoice with those who have been sent to it, under the guidance of Christ the Lord, to His glory; and by its writings and memorials makes these men known to those who follow so that "they may set their hope in God and not forget the works of God but keep His commandments."[2] It is therefore proper for us, too, with the help of the Lord and to the best of our ability, to make mention of our master and write about him whom we, with the rest of the world, can call Saint Gregory.[3]

Here ends our brief preface.

[Chapter 1]

Gregory was Roman by nationality, his father being Gordianus and his mother Sylvia;[4] so he was noble in the eyes of the law but nobler still in heart in the sight of God because of his religious life.[5] He lived for a long time in a monastery where, as he himself declares, all transitory affairs were of little importance to his mind. He rose above passing events and accustomed himself to think about nothing but heavenly themes.[6]

[Chapter 2]

We can clearly appreciate from his words, even though only partially and imperfectly, how he reached this state

eum in eo loco honorificum secundum apostolicę ubi hec designat clare Constantinopolim testantur responsa, ubi confestim non in hoc gloriando, sed solite se humiliando, "Diu," inquit, "longeque conversationis gratiam distuli. Et

p. 76 postquam / cęlesti sum[1] desiderio afflatus, sęculari habitu contegi melius putavi. Aperiebatur enim mihi aeternitatis amore quod quererem, sed inolita me consuetudo devinxerat, ne exteriorem cultum mutarem." Deinde cogente se animo presenti mundo servire, multa se dicit ex eius cura succrescere.[2] Que tandem cuncta sollicite fugiens, portum monasterii petisse ex huius vite naufragio nudus evadens. Tunc celeriter[3] humilitatis exemplo usus gratissimo dixit, "Quia enim plerumque navem incaute religatam, etiam de sinu tuti littoris excutit, cum tempestas excrescit, repente me sub pretextu ecclesiastici ordinis, in curarum secularium[4] pelago reperi[5] quietem monasterii, quia habendo non fortiter tenui, quam stricte tenenda fuerit, perdendo cognovi." Ergo post hec sibi oboedientię virtus opponi dicebat ad percipiendum sacri altaris ministerium. "Postque hoc nolenti," ait,[6] "mihi atque renitenti cum grave esset altaris ministerium, etiam pondus est cure pastoralis iniunctum. Quod tanto nunc[7] durius tolero, quanto me ei imparem sentiens, in nulla fiducie consolatione respiro." De quo paulo post tempore quo ad ministerium inquit, "altaris

---

[1] summi *M1*   [2] ce over erasure *M1*   [3] ins. sollicite *M1*. Om. ed.   [4-5] ed. pelagus raperet *M1*   [6] above *M2*   [7] tunc *M1*

of mind. In the first place these writings bear witness to the fact that he was an honourable representative of the apostolic see in the place which he explicitly states was Constantinople.[7] In these passages he speaks straightforwardly, not indeed boastingly but with his habitual humility, about this matter: "For a long time," he says, "I put far from me the grace of godly living: and even after I had been inspired with heavenly longings, I thought it better to wear the secular habit. For though the way of attaining what I sought in my desire for heavenly things was revealed to me, yet inveterate habits bound me so that I could not change my outer way of life." Then he adds that, because his heart compelled him to serve this present world, his cares were thereby greatly increased. So, eagerly fleeing from all these things, he sought the haven of a monastery[8] and escaped naked from the shipwreck of this life. Thereupon, still making use of this charming yet humble simile,[9] he hastened to add that, just as when a storm arises it drags a carelessly moored ship even from the lee of a sheltering shore, "so," he says, "I suddenly found myself, though wearing the dress of an ecclesiastical order, tossed in the waves of secular cares and losing the peace of the monastery because, when I had it, I did not hang on to it as firmly as I should have done." After this he says he was called upon, being faced with the duty of obedience, to undertake the ministry of the sacred altar. "And after this," he adds, "unwilling and reluctant though I was, since the ministry of the altar was in itself a heavy load, the weight of pastoral care was added to my burden. And now I endure it with the greater difficulty because I feel myself unequal to it and I have no self-confidence to encourage or refresh me. So," he said, "a little time after I had under-

accessi hoc me ignorante actum est, ut sacri ordinis pondus acciperem; ubi me[8] scilicet multi ex monasterio fratres mei, germana vincti[9] caritate secuti sunt. Quod divina effectum / dispensatione conspicerem, ut eorum semper exemplo ad orationis placidum[10] litus, quasi anchore fune restringerer cum causarum secularium incessabili [11]inpulsu fluctuarem.[12] Ad illorum quippe consortium, velut ad tutissimi[13] portus sinum, terreni actus flumina fluctusque fugiebam. Et licet illud me ministerium ex monasterio abstractum, a pristine quietis vita mucrone sue occupationis extinxerat, inter eos tamen per studiose lectionis[14] alloquium, cottidiana me aspiratio conpuctionis animabat."

[*Chapter 3*]
Cum enim de his dixisse ista sufficere credimus, ad ea que sequuntur[1] festinemus, qualiter doctor noster sanctus Gregorius vir ceteris incomparabilis sit, nobis in sanctitate Deo adiuvante, venerandus. De quo librum scribere cupientes cum pauca eius de gestis audivimus signorum, nec fastidium sit legentibus precamur, si aliquid de laude tanti viri loquamur uberius. Multi igitur a miraculis vitam quidem sanctorum solent considerare, atque a signis sancta illorum merita metiri, et hoc nec inmerito. Nam sepe eos Deus qui est mirabilis in sanctis suis quos pre ceteris amat, iam miraculis facit coruscare pre ceteris.

[*Chapter 4*]
Unde nostrorum nonnulli mirabilem[1] virum sanctum Gre-

---

[8] *above* M2   [9] victi *M1*   [10] *ed.* placitum *M1*   [11-12] *ed. over erasure* inpulsa fluctuum *M2*   [13] *ed.* tutisimi *M1*   [14] *ed.* letionis *M1*   [1] [c. 3] *ed.* secuntur *M1*   [1] [c. 4] vir *inserted and erased*

Gregory the Great

taken the ministry of the altar, it was decided without my knowledge that I should receive the burden of a sacred office. Many of the brethren from my monastery, compelled by brotherly love, followed me. I saw that this had happened by divine dispensation, so that, through their unremitting example, I could bind myself, as it were by an anchor cable, to the calm shores of prayer; while being tossed about by the ceaseless tide of secular business, I fled to their fellowship as to the refuge of a safe port from the currents and waves of earthly affairs. And though this office of mine had dragged me from the monastery and, with the distraction of business, had cut me off as with a knife from my former life of quiet, yet by my serious conferences and readings with them, I was daily stirred to a desire for devotion."[10]

[Chapter 3]

As in our opinion we have said enough about these matters, we will hasten on to what follows and, with the help of God, consider how far our holy teacher the incomparable Gregory ought to be honoured by us as a saint. We wish to write a book about him, though, in the record of his deeds, we have heard of few miracles: but we pray our readers not to feel distaste[11] if we praise the great man somewhat exuberantly. For many are accustomed to judge the lives of saints by their miracles and to measure their merits and holiness by the signs they perform; nor is this unreasonable; for often God, who is glorious in his saints[12] that he loves beyond other men, makes them shine above other men by the miracles they perform.

[Chapter 4]

Therefore some of our people rightly suppose that this

gorium papam Romanum, et ut ita dicam, apostolicum, signis divinis apte suspicantur, que et mira dicuntur / merito fulsisse. Quibus etiam est pure agnoscendum,[2] quia ut ille sanctus vir, "Sunt," inquit, "plerique qui, etsi[3] signa non faciunt, signa tamen facientibus dispares non sunt." Hinc namque de signis proprię virtutis suę quas fecit Veritas, a se minoribus maiora id est apostolis concessa divinis ostendit, maiora horum facietis. Eos quoque non esse omnibus per merita maiores, alibi testantur, ubi de Johanne Baptista inter natos[4] maior non surrexisse dicebat. Quem nequaquam talia ut apostolus signa fecisse didicimus, eum tamen potuisse talia non dubitamus. Si ita ei convenirent ut illis, vel si fecisset humanam excederet naturam, dum tam sancte pre ceteris conceptus est et natus, que[5] etiam ad idola distruenda infidelium paganorum, vel fidelium aliquando fidem infirmam confirmandam concessa sunt; illorum maxime doctoribus, unde et ibi eo sepius mirabiliusque declarantur, quo fiunt ipsi doctores meliores. Hinc igitur quidam heremite[6] viri maxime latentes, nullis declarantur[7] miraculis, at contra minores in urbibus multa sepe fecere miracula. Sunt in his nonnulli qui[8] animabus per doctrinam non valde prodesse[9] inveniuntur, unde sunt nonnulli qui scilicet hic suam percipientes

---

[2] anoscendum *M1*   [3] *ed.* et *M1*   [4] nato *M1*   [5] *above M2*   [6] hemite *M1*
[7] *ed.* declarare *M1*   [8] *above M2*   [9] procedisse *M1*

wonderful man St. Gregory, the Pope of Rome and, if I may say so, the apostolic Pope,[13] deservedly gained renown by holy signs which can even be called miracles. Such men clearly recognize that there are many, like this holy man, who, as Gregory himself said, do not perform miracles but are not unequal to those who do.[14] For He, the Truth,[15] showed that in the matter of signs which He performed by His own power, it was granted to lesser men than Himself, namely the holy Apostles, to do greater— "Greater works than these shall ye do."[16] Further He showed elsewhere that the Apostles were not greater than all other men by their merits; when speaking of John the Baptist, he said, "Among them that are born of women there hath not risen a greater."[17] Yet we have never heard that John did such miracles as any of the Apostles did, though we do not doubt that he could have done such. If miracles had been appropriate for him as they were for the Apostles, then in performing them he would have overstepped the bounds of human nature, seeing that his conception and birth were holier than those of others. Miracles are granted for the destruction of the idols of unbelieving pagans, or sometimes to confirm the weak faith of believers; most of all, they are granted to those who instruct the pagans, and so, the more gloriously and frequently they are manifested in those lands, the more convincing they become as teachers. Hence some hermits, though very great men, living obscure lives, are not revealed by any miracles, but, on the contrary, lesser men living in cities have often performed many miracles. There are men in these places who find that they cannot successfully benefit souls just by preaching; hence some of them, perceiving in this power a certain recompense for all their toil, begin to

p. 79 mercedem, quomodo[10] queruntque in dato falso / ut gloriantur signorum, ita etiam et in doctrina. Non enim in viscerato medullitus fervore venarum, rivulos sugentes, gustant divinitatis, qui a pręceptorum deviantes custodia,[11] ea quę minime faciunt predicant. Et sunt nonulli qui cum infidelibus signa petunt sicut ait apostolus, "Iudei signa petunt, quibus signum Ionę Christus comminatur futurum." Et iterum,[12] "Lingue in signum sunt, non fidelibus sed infidelibus, [13]profetię autem non infidelibus[14] sed fidelibus,"[15] qui cum in ecclesia Christi sanctorum solent semper natalicios maximos[16] celebrare dies, quibus in vitam morientes nascunter ęternam Patri in perpetuum filii coheredes Christi.

[*Chapter 5*]
De nostro igitur magistro beato Gregorio ea quę nobiscum ab antiquis fama sanctitatis eius a diversis notavit referamus. In quibus etiam perpauca de multis nos audisse credimus, in eis tantum de hoc clarissime fame viro signa sanctitatis qui requirunt, his possunt agnoscere satis evidenter indiciis. Sunt ergo nonnulli, et ut verius dicam, fuere ante nos, qui tanta iam per Spiritum sanctum fulgebant doctrina, ut innumerabiles per mundum illorum inrigati imbribus verborum fructum adferunt in patientia, imitatores eius qui tradidit semetipsum pro nobis oblationem et hostiam Deo in odorem suavitatis. Inter quos

---

[10] quando *M1* [11] custodiam *M1* [12] item *M1* [13–15] *in margin M2* [14] *ed.* fi cut away in margin [16] maximas *M1*

boast of their miracles as well as of their teaching, relying falsely on this gift. But those who depart from their duty of keeping those precepts and do not practise what they preach, fail to taste the streams of divine life or to draw them into the pulsing flow of the veins beneath the flesh. There are some too who, like the unbelievers, seek after signs; as the Apostle says, "The Jews require a sign," and Christ threatens them with the sign of Jonah which was to come. And again we read, "Tongues are for a sign, not to them that believe but to them that believe not: but prophesying serveth, not for them that believe not but for them that believe"[18] who are accustomed always to celebrate in the Church of Christ as their greatest festival days the birthdays[19] of the saints on which they died to this life and were born to the Father into the life everlasting, as His sons for ever and as joint-heirs with Christ.[20]

[Chapter 5]

Let us therefore relate those facts about our blessed master Gregory which the fame of his holiness has preserved amongst us, derived from various sources and from ancient times. Of these facts we realize that we have heard only a very few out of many; but any who are only looking for such miracles as prove the sanctity of this renowned man, can find the proof clearly enough in this evidence. There are some now and, indeed, there have been some before our time who, through the Holy Spirit, were so conspicuous by their teaching that innumerable people throughout the world have been revived by the refreshing showers of their words and "bring forth fruit with patience," becoming imitators of Him who "gave Himself for us, an offering and a sacrifice to God for a sweet-smelling savour."[21] Among these we number Gregory, this

apostolicum nostrum sanctum Gregorium virum prefatum adnumeramus,[1] utinam et nos cum illo.

[Chapter 6]

Juxta cuius sententiam quando omnes apostoli, suas secum provincias ducentes / Domino in die iudicii ostendent, atque singuli gentium doctores, nos ille, id est gentem Anglorum,[1] eo miratius per se gratia Dei credimus edoctam adducere,[2] quo[3] eam corpore absens sed tantum spiritu presens, apostolica divinitus potestate eius audacter, fortis nimirum viri [4]eius quem[5] Christus alligavit domum ingrediens, vasa eius quę nos fuimus, aliquando tenebre, nunc autem lux in Domino, diripiebat. Unde cum mira quę unus atque idem spiritus operatur in omnibus, dividens singulis prout vult, veraciter quę iam sint requiramus, invenimus, non in salvatione tantum agnoscenda corporum vel suscitatione mortuorum, sed ut iste iam sanctus tractavit[6] noster Gregorius, eo plus animarum quo in illis imago Dei sumus, quę factura creati in Christo Iesu operibus bonis quę preparavit Deus ut in illis ambulemus. De his igitur quę diversis crismatum donis desursum perfecta[7] a patre luminum descendunt[8] ita dicit[9] apostolus, unicuique autem nostram data est gratia per mensuram donationis Christi. De qua iterum alii sermonem sapientię, alii scientię[10] datam esse dicit[11], fidem quoque et gratiam sanitatum, et cetera, que pro mirabili[12] usu plus habentur hominibus qui in faciem iudicant, quam ei qui in corde, Deus qui in beato Gregorio illa iam maiora per sermonem

---

[1] [c. 5] adnumeramur *M1*   [1] [c. 6] *crossed* l *M1*   [2] *first* d *above M2*   [3] aquo *M1*   [4-5] usque *M1*   [6] cratavit? *M1*   [7] perfectam *M1*   [8] discendunt *M1*   [9] *ed.* dict *M1*   [10-11] *in margin M1, original text erased*   [12] mirabile *M1*

apostolic saint of ours, and would that we might be numbered with him.

[Chapter 6]

According to Gregory's opinion, when all the Apostles bring their own peoples with them and each individual teacher brings his own race to present them to the Lord in the Day of Judgment, he will bring us—that is, the English people—instructed by him through God's grace;[22] and we believe this to be all the more wonderful because, though absent in the body yet present in the spirit, through his divinely given apostolic powers he bravely entered the house of the strong man whom Christ had bound, taking as spoil those goods, that is, ourselves, who were "sometimes darkness but now are light in the Lord." So when we seek to know what those marvels truly are which "one and the selfsame Spirit worketh, dividing to every man severally as he wills,"[23] we find that they are to be recognized not only in the healing of the body or the raising from the dead, but, as our own St. Gregory has explained,[24] still more in the healing of souls, because it is in them that we are the image of God, "His workmanship, created in Christ Jesus unto good works that we should walk in them." Of these various gifts of grace which "come down perfect from the Father of Lights" the Apostle speaks thus, "To every one of us is given according to the measure of the gift of Christ." Of these he says that "to one is given the word of wisdom, to another the word of knowledge," as well as "faith and gifts of healing";[25] and there are other gifts which are considered more marvelous still in the eyes of men who judge by appearance than in the eyes of Him who judges the heart[26]—namely, God, who reveals in the blessed Gregory still greater wonders through the words of

p. 81 sapientię[13] et scientię Christi Iesu declarat. / Unde ipse de istis in eius loquitur evangelii omeliis dicens, "Quę nimirum miracula tanto maiora sunt quanto spiritalia": et iterum, "que tanto securiora sunt quanto spiritalia." Et hoc contra eos qui gloriantur in signis, et illic[14] audituri sunt, "Discedite a me omnes qui operamini[15] iniquitatem." Plus igitur nobis Christus per sanctum loquendo proficit Gregorium, quam quod Petrum apostolum per undas fecit ambulare[16], vel quod per Paulum eius co-apostolum cecitate malignum percussit magum.

[*Chapter 7*]

Nam cum dixit, "Discite[1] a me quia mitis sum et humilis corde," quod nos discere beatus docuit Gregorius, non post Petrum per maria ambulare vel mortuos suscitare. Et cum iterum ait, "In pacientia vestra possidebitis animas vestras," cuius nos virtutem signis et miraculis maiorem esse cognoscere, sanctus docuit agnoscendo Gregorius. Vilior itaque vis est que stuporem semper visu et auditu solet incutere cognitum, quam quod mitem Christum et humilem simul et caritatem quę ipse est habet in perpetuum. Huius igitur exemplum qui est principium rerum omnium, primum ponimus de hoc viro signum sanctitatis. Ad hec ubi illum imitando quante humilitatis horum immo omnes eius pre-
p. 82 ceptorum / fuerit doctor noster statim agnoscitur, per quam maior esse in regno cęlorum ipse Christus apostolis suis interrogantibus quis ibi sit maior, respondit humilem. Nam cum ad curam pastoralem prefatam apostolicę dignitatis a populo Dei electus est, tam eam humiliter aufugit,

---

[13] *ed.* sapientientię *M1*   [14] illinc *M1*   [15] operantur *M1*   [16] ambure *M1*
[1] discedite *M1*

the wisdom and knowledge of Christ Jesus.[27] This is how he deals with the subject in his *Homilies on the Gospels:* "Miracles," he says, "are the greater, the more spiritual they are"; and, again, "If they are spiritual they are so much the surer."[28] These, too, are his words against those who boast of their wonderful works here and who there are going to hear from Him, "Depart from me all ye workers of iniquity." Therefore Christ avails us more as He speaks through St. Gregory than when He made the Apostle Peter walk on the waves; or when through Peter's fellow-Apostle Paul He struck the evil magician with blindness.[29]

[Chapter 7]

When Christ said, "Learn of me for I am meek and lowly in heart," the blessed Gregory explained to us that we were not to learn to walk over the waves after Peter or raise the dead. Again, when He says, "In your patience possess ye your souls,"[30] St. Gregory taught us to recognize that this virtue is greater than signs or miracles.[31] So that power which can only produce amazement inspired by what is seen and heard is of a baser kind than that which avails itself of the meek and lowly Christ and the love which Christ Himself ever has. Therefore we place first as a sign of the sanctity of this man the fact that he followed the example of Him who is the beginning of all things. So when we imitate a man of such great humility, we at once accept him as our teacher in these precepts—nay, in all the precepts of Christ; for it was Christ Himself who, when His Apostles asked Him who was the greatest in the Kingdom of Heaven, answered that it was the meek.[32] So when Gregory was elected by the people of God to the pastoral office and the apostolic dignity already mentioned, he fled

ut ubi se potuisset abscondere satis anxie querebat. Qui cum fuisset tanta servatus cura ut iam porte urbis qua inerat passim custodibus cingebantur,² dicitur a negotiatoribus se obtinuisse³ ut in cratere occultatus educeretur. Sicque statim silve avias querendo latebras, interseruit se frondissimis⁴ fruticum opacis occultandum. Ubi cum fuisset tribus diebus et noctibus, eum etiam portarum vigiles cęlestium, confestim quo erat declamabant. Cum populus Dei non alterum pro eo ut dilexit elegit, sed ut ille monstraretur ab eo, ieiuniis et orationibus illis diebus ac noctibus serviens, diligenter precatus est. Nam visa est omnibus per totas ⁵tres noctes⁶ columna lucidissima silvam intrasse, porrecto cacumine usque ad celum. Que cuidam sancto viro quem anachoretam⁷ fuisse audivimus visa est scala, et
p. 83 descendentes per eam et⁸ ascendentes angeli / sicut⁹ de beato Iacob in Luza legimus, quę ex inde Bethel, hoc est domus Dei¹⁰ vocata¹¹ est. De qua celeriter, "non est hic," ait, "aliud nisi domus Dei et porta cęli." Sanctus igitur de quo loquimur Gregorius, cum posuit tenebras latibulum suum, in circuitu eius, tamen etiam in tabernaculum domus Dei posita, confestim super candelabrum lucerna omnibus in ea lucebat. Cum declaratus ubi latebat inventus, ductus est ad sacerdotium. "Plerique," ait sanctus Heronimus, "ad sacerdotium erecti quanto plus pro animi humilitate repugnant, tanto magis in se omni¹² studio¹³ concitant, eoque

---

² cingæbantur *M1*   ³ obtenuisse *M1*   ⁴ ed. fromdissimis *M1*   ⁵⁻⁶ noctes tres *M1*   ⁷ anachoritam *M1*   ⁸ above *M2*   ⁹ in margin *M2*   ¹⁰ above *M1*   ¹¹ vocatus *M1*   ¹² *original reading erased:* omni above *M2*   ¹³ ed. studia *M1*

from it with great humility[33] and very anxiously sought a place to hide in. But he was watched with such care that even the entrance gates of the city were surrounded by guards on every side; so he is said to have persuaded some merchants to take him out, hidden in a cask. He then immediately sought out a hiding-place in the depths of the woods, thrusting himself into the leafiest shades of the bushes, where he lay hidden. But after he had been there for three days and nights, the watchmen at the heavenly gates forthwith declared his whereabouts. For the people of God did not elect someone else, as he had hoped, but gave themselves up to fasting and supplication day and night,[34] praying earnestly that God would show them where he was. Then for three whole nights there appeared to them a very bright column of light which penetrated the forest so that its top reached up to the sky. It appeared in the form of a ladder to a certain holy man who was an anchorite, or so we have heard, with angels descending and ascending on it, as we read of the blessed Jacob at Luz, the place which, from this incident, came to be called Bethel—that is, the house of God. Jacob immediately said of it that "this is none other but the house of God and this is the gate of heaven." So the same St. Gregory, though he "made darkness his secret place round about him," nevertheless, when once he had been placed in the tabernacle of the house of God, shone forth like a lamp upon its stand to all who were in the house.[35] When his hiding-place was revealed, he was found and led to the sacred office. St. Jerome says[36] of those who are promoted to a sacred office that the more they resist it because of their humility of spirit, the more they arouse themselves to every exertion and become the worthier in proportion as they declare

digniores fiunt quo se fatentur indignos"; et hoc merito. Nam eius qui sacerdos et hostia pro nobis esse dignatus est, Christi magistri sequuntur exemplum, qui in Patris sui oboedientia humiliatus est usque ad mortem, mortem autem crucis. Rex fieri noluit, sed cum, inquit, venerunt ut raperent eum sibi regem, quo cognito fugit Iesus et abscondit se ab eis. Et iterum quando ad principatum regni cęlestis a Patre pro mundi oblatus est salute, eadem humilitate pro se precatus est dicens, "Pater, si fieri potest, transeat a me calix iste."

[*Chapter 8*]

Tunc etiam Patris sui perfectam secutus voluntatem, velut invitus quodam modo corpore inventus, ductus est ad *p. 84* sacerdotium pro nobis / obediens[1] ad crucem ut eam eius exemplo[2] portantes qui prius totius plebis[3] regnum refugit, fugitivum ac terrenum, crucifixus adeptus est imperium; humilis et mitis pro inimicis orando se ipsum obtulit pro omnibus, in quo illum qui sequitur, licet undis submersus, maior erit in cęlo. Quod sanctus implendo docuit nos Gregorius dicens, "Pro inimico nihil postulat, qui pro eo ex caritate non orat," ut perfecta ex hoc fiat in nobis Christi caritas sine qua apostolus catalogum enumerando virtutum, si eas omnes haberet, nihil se esse testatur. Vere ergo de viro hoc a Domino dicitur, "Lex veritatis fuit in ore eius, et iniquitas non est inventa in labiis eius," et reliqua. Unde

---

[1] obedientem *M1*   [2] *in margin M1*   [3] *ed.* plebem *M1*

Gregory the Great 89

their own unworthiness; and properly so, for they are following the example of their master Christ, who deigned to be both priest and sacrifice for us; who humbled himself unto death in obedience to His Father, even the death of the cross. He did not wish to be king, but when, as the Scripture relates, they came to take him by force to make Him king, Jesus perceived it and fled and hid himself from them. Again when He was offered up by His Father to take the chief place in the Kingdom of Heaven for the salvation of the world, He prayed for Himself with the same humility, "Father, if it be possible, let this cup pass from me."[37]

[Chapter 8]

Then, following His Father's perfect will and being found, as it were unwillingly, in bodily form, He was led to the fulfilment of His priestly office when He became obedient to the cross for our sakes; and we too bear our cross after His example. He who first shunned the kingdom of the whole world, a fleeting, earthly kingdom, gained an empire when He was crucified; humble and meek, He offered Himself for all, even praying for His enemies. And this is the way whereby he who follows Him, even though the waves go over him, will be very great in heaven. St. Gregory taught us by his own practice as well as by his words that "he asks nothing for his enemy who does not pray for him out of love,"[38] so that in this way the love of Christ may be made perfect in us—that love without which, as the Apostle testifies when enumerating a whole catalogue of the virtues, even though we have all the rest we have nothing. It was surely of this man that the Lord was speaking when he said, "The law of truth was in his mouth and iniquity was not found in his

eum utique preceptum Domini lucidum inluminans oculos, sic inluminavit ut inter multa ingenii munimina suę in signum sanctitatis ad gratiam prophęte singulari fertur dono de nobis intellegentię pervenisse.

[*Chapter 9*]

Quod omnino non est tegendum silentio, quam spiritaliter ad Deum quomodoque cordis inconparabili speculo oculorum nostram providendo propagavit ad Deum conversionem. Est igitur narratio fidelium, ante predictum eius pontificatum, Roman venisse quidam de nostra natione forma et crinibus candidati albis. Quos cum audisset venisse, iam dilexit vidisse eosque alme[1] mentis intuitu sibi adscitos, recenti / specię inconsueta suspensus et, quod maximum est, Deo intus admonente, cuius gentis fuissent, inquisivit. Quos quidam pulchros fuisse pueros dicunt et quidam vero crispos iuvenes et decoros. Cumque responderent, "Anguli dicuntur, illi de quibus sumus," ille dixit, "Angeli Dei." Deinde dixit, "Rex gentis illius, quomodo nominatur?" Et dixerunt, "Aelli." Et ille ait, "Alleluia. Laus enim Dei esse debet illic." Tribus quoque illius nomen de qua[2] erant proprię[3] requisivit. Et dixerunt, "Deirę." Et ille dixit, "De ira Dei confugientes ad fidem."

[*Chapter 10*]

Tam itaque spiritali data occasione inflammatus, precessorem pontificatus sui papam Benedictum tam inhianter

---
[1] *ed.* albe *M1*   [2] quo *M1*   [3] *ed.* proprę *M1*

Gregory the Great

lips," and so on. So, "the pure commandment of the Lord enlightening his eyes"[39] enlightened him to such an extent that amid the many strong points in his character, it is said that, as a sign of holiness, he attained to the grace of prophecy,[40] shown in his unique gift that enabled him to understand our needs.

[Chapter 9]

So we must not pass over in silence how, through the Spirit of God and with the incomparable discernment of his inward eye, he foresaw and made provision for our conversion to God. There is a story told by the faithful[41] that, before he became Pope, there came to Rome certain people of our nation, fair-skinned and light-haired. When he heard of their arrival he was eager to see them; being prompted by a fortunate intuition, being puzzled by their new and unusual appearance, and, above all, being inspired by God, he received them and asked what race they belonged to. (Now some say they were beautiful boys, while others say that they were curly-haired, handsome youths.) They answered, "The people we belong to are called Angles."[42] "Angels of God," he replied. Then he asked further, "What is the name of the king of that people?" They said, "Ælli," whereupon he said, "Alleluia, God's praise must be heard there."[43] Then he asked the name of their own tribe, to which they answered, "Deire,"[44] and he replied, "They shall flee from the wrath of God to the faith."

[Chapter 10]

Gregory was so greatly moved by the spiritual opportunity presented to him that he begged Pope Benedict,[45] his predecessor in the pontificate, so insistently to give him

huc proficiscendi pręcatus est dedisse licentiam, ut precis[1] sue non potuit declinare nimietatem, illo dicente, "Miserum, tam pulchris vasis infernus debuisse repleri." Hec et his similia illo dicente, licentiam[2] tribuit pontifex huc[3] iter agendi. Ex qua iam licentia populum satis contristavit Romanum. Unde tale dicitur condictum fecisse, ut se in tres partes dividendo iuxta viam qua profectus est ad eclesiam [4]sancti Petri[5] idem pontifex, unaquaque autem pars eo transiente, sic proclamavit ad eum, "Petrum offendisti: Romam / destruxisti: Gregorium dimisisti." His ergo tam terribiliter tercio audiens, concite post missis legatis fecit eum reverti. Cuius reversionis prius, Domino in se loquente sancta mente per unam locustam agnovit iterationem. Confecto namque trium dierum itinere, quiescentibus illis quodam loco, ut iter agentibus moris est, venit ad eum locusta[6] legentem[7]. E cuius nomine statim quasi sibi diceret, "Sta in loco," agnovit, concite tamen ortatus est comites parare se ad proficiscendum. Quod dum agebat cum illis, pręventus a nuntiis, reductus est Romę.

[*Chapter 11*]

Postque non multum tempus papa defuncto, electus, ut prescripsimus, ad pontificatum est; quantaque[1] potuit festinatione venerandę memorię viros huc, Augustinum et Mellitum atque Laurentium direxit cum ceteris, Augustinum ordinando episcopum, a quo hic Mellitus dicitur et a Mellito Laurentius ordinatus.

---

[1] [c. 10] *ed.* preces *M1*   [2] lincentiam *M1*   [3] hoc *M1*   [4-5] *in margin M1*
[6] *above M2*   [7] logentem *M1*   [1] [c. 11] que *above M2*

Gregory the Great

permission to set out for our land that the Pope could not refuse his urgent prayer. "It would be a wretched thing," cried Gregory, "for hell to be filled with such lovely vessels."[46] As he pleaded with such words as these, the Pope gave him permission to make the journey here. But the Romans were greatly perturbed because the Pope had granted his request. So when it was announced that permission had been given, they divided themselves into three groups and stood along the road by which the Pope went to St. Peter's Church; as he passed, each group shouted at him, "You have offended Peter, you have destroyed Rome, you have sent Gregory away."[47] As soon as he heard their dreadful cry for the third time, he quickly sent messengers after Gregory to make him return. But Gregory, with holy insight, had already learned of this repeated call for his return through the inward promptings of the Lord and by means of a locust. For after a three days' journey, while they were resting in a certain place as travelers are accustomed to do, a locust settled on him while he was reading. At once he recognized from the name of the insect that he was, as it were, being told to stay in the place;[48] nevertheless he quickly urged his comrades to move on. But as he was doing so, he was forestalled by the messengers and he and his companions were brought back to Rome.

[Chapter 11]

Not long afterwards the Pope died and, as we have already said, Gregory was elected to the pontificate.[49] With as little delay as possible he sent here Augustine, Mellitus, and Laurentius, men of honoured memory, together with others, having consecrated Augustine bishop. Mellitus is said to have been consecrated here by Augustine and Laurentius by Mellitus.[50]

[Chapter 12]

Per hos igitur regum omnium[1] primus Angulorum[2] Edilbertus rex Cantuariorum ad fidem Christi correctus, eius baptismo dealbatus cum sua enituit natione. Post hunc in gente nostra, quę dicitur Humbrensium, Eduinus, Aelli prefati filius, quem sub vaticinatione alleluiatica laudationis divinę non inmerito meminimus,[3] / rex precepit tam sapientia singularis quam etiam sceptro dicionis regię, a tempore quo gens Angulorum[4] hanc ingreditur insulam.

[Chapter 13]

O quam pulchre quamque hec omnia decenter[1] simul sibi conveniunt prefata. Ergo nomen Angulorum,[2] si una e littera addetur, angelorum sonat; pro certo vocabulum quorum proprium est semper omnipotentem Deum in celis laudare, et non deficere, quia non lassescunt in laude. Quos beatus Iohannes, in Apocalipsin testatur voce exercitus celestis vidisse et audisse, tamquam vocem aquarum multarum et tamquam vocem validorum tonitruorum dicentium alleluia. Cuius sacramenti sanctitas inmutabilis esse, in perpetuum omnibus sanctis sciendum est, sicut et illi in contemplatione deitatis[3] effecti sunt, quorum per illud indeficiens est laudatio eius in ecclesia sanctorum. Cuius expositio[4] duorum habet interpretationem verborum,[5] hoc est laus Dei. Et Aelli duabus compositum est sillabis quarum in priori cum e littera adsumitur et in sequenti pro i ponitur e[6], all[7] vocatur, quod in nostra lingua omnes[8] absolute indicat. Et hoc est quod ait Dominus noster, "Venite

---

[1] [c. 12] nium *above* M2   [2] n *above* M2   [3] me *above* M2   [4] u *expunged* M2
[1] [c. 13] decentur M1   [2] u *expunged* M2   [3] *ed.* deytatis M1   [4] expotio M1
[5] verborum *repeated in margin* M1   [6] *above* M1   [7] *crossed* l's M1   [8] omnibus M2

[Chapter 12]

The first of all the kings of England to be led to faith in Christ by these men was Æthelberht, King of Kent, who shone forth with all his nation after he had been cleansed in the waters of baptism.[51] After him came Edwin, a man of this race of ours which is called the Humbrians. He was the son of Ælli, whom we have very rightly mentioned in connection with that prophetic Alleluia of divine praise. From the time when the English race came to this island, King Edwin held the pre-eminence as much for the wisdom as for the extent of his royal and single-handed sway.[52]

[Chapter 13]

How beautifully and, at the same time, how appropriately do all these matters fit in with one another. Thus the name of the Angli, with the addition of the single letter *e,* means angels, as those beings are called whose property is always to praise Almighty God in heaven and that without ceasing, because they never tire in their praises. St. John in the Apocalypse bears witness that he both saw and heard them, having the voice of a celestial army, "as the voice of many waters and as the voice of mighty thunderings, saying Alleluia."[53] And all the saints must know that this holy ministry is changeless and endless; just as they themselves have likewise been moved to cry "alleluia," in the contemplation of the Deity, so His praise shall never cease in the congregation of the saints.[54] The meaning of "alleluia" can be put into two words—God's praise. And *Ælli* is made up of two syllables: if in the first syllable we take away the *e* and in the second replace *i* by *e,* it becomes "alle," which in our language means absolutely all. And this is just what our Lord says, "Come unto me, *all* ye that labour and are

ad me omnes qui laboratis et onerati estis," et reliqua. Si[9] regem quoque significat alle Patrem, lu Filium, ia Spiritum Sanctum.

[Chapter 14]

p. 88 Porro cum in lumbis fortasse cum / hoc fuit vaticinatum adhuc patris sui Aelli fuit predestinatum[1] vas misericordię Deo Eduinus, cuius nomen tribus sillabis constans, recte sibi designat sancte misterium trinitatis, quod ille docebat qui omnes ad se invitat baptizatos in nomine Patris et Filii et Spiritus sancti. Huius namque Eduini pater in baptismo venerandus fuit Paulinus antistes, unus illorum quos inter nos[2] direxit, ut diximus, Gregorius: qui tam facile signum Dei sui sapientię quadam ut reor dominica dicitur dedisse.

[Chapter 15]

Cum stipatus ad eclesiam rex prefatus ad caticuminum eorum qui adhuc erant[1] gentilitati non solum, sed etiam et non licitis stricti coniugiis,[2] cum illo festinavit ab aula ubi prius adhuc utrumque emendandum hortati sunt ab illis, dum quedam stridula cornix ad plagam voce peiorem[3] cantavit. Tunc omnis multitudo regia quę adhuc erat in platea populi, audiens[4] avem, stupore ad eam conversa subsistit, quasi illud canticum novum carmen Deo nostro non esset vero[5] futurum in eclesia, sed falso ad nihil utile. Tunc venerandus episcopus puero suo cuidam, Deo omnia ex arce sua speculante providentequę, "Dirige,"[6] inquit, "sagittam in avem otius." Quo festinanter effecto, avis sagittam servari precepit[7] usque dum, peracto catacuminio[8] /

---

[9] ad *inserted and erased* M1 [1] [c. 14] *ed*. prædistinatum M1 [2] s *over erasure* M2 [1] [c. 15] *above* M2 [2] coniugis M1 [3] peorem M1 [4] a iudeis M1 [5] vere M1 [6] dirigetur (?) M1 [7] preepit M1 [8] cacuminio M1

heavy laden,"⁵⁵ and so on. Though it is the name of a king, *alle* also signifies the Father, *lu* the Son, and *ia* the Holy Spirit.

[Chapter 14]

Further, when the prophecy was made, Edwin, predestined to be a "vessel of mercy" for God, was perhaps still in the loins of his father Ælli. Edwin's name,⁵⁶ consisting of three syllables, truly signifies the mystery of the Holy Trinity which He taught, inviting all to come to Him and be baptized in the name of the Father, the Son, and the Holy Spirit.⁵⁷

[Chapter 15]

Now Edwin's godfather at his baptism was the reverend Bishop Paulinus,⁵⁸ one of those whom, as we have said, Gregory sent us. He is said, on a certain Sunday I believe it was, to have given very promptly a sign of his God-given wisdom. King Edwin was hurrying to the church to receive instruction, surrounded by a crowd of those who were still bound not only to heathenism but also to unlawful wives;⁵⁹ they had left the hall where they had been exhorted to put both these matters right when a crow set up a hoarse croaking from an unpropitious quarter of the sky.⁶⁰ Thereupon the whole of the royal company, who were still in the public square, heard the bird and turned towards it, halting in amazement as if they believed that the "new song" in the church was not to be "praise unto our God," but something false and useless.⁶¹ Then, while God looked down from his heaven and guided everything, the reverend bishop said to one of his youths, "Shoot the bird down quickly with an arrow." This was speedily done and then the bishop told him that the arrow from the bird

p. 89 eorum qui erant catezizandi, asportatur[9] in aulam. Omnibusque illuc congregatis recenti rudoque adhuc populo Dei bene satis eo causam donante, confirmavit antiquum[10] scelus[11] nomen idolatrię, tam evidenti signo esse pro nihilo in[12] omnibus discendum, dicens etiam sibi ipsi avis illa insensata mortem cavere cum nescisset, immo renatis ad imaginem Dei baptizatis omnino hominibus, qui dominantur piscibus maris et volatilibus cęli atque universis animantibus terrę, nihil profuturum prenuntiet, quas illi ex sua subtili natura ad deceptionem stultorum se scire, Deo iuste permittente, iactitant.

[*Chapter 16*]
Sed quia regis nostri christianissimi facimus Eduini mentionem, dignum fuit etiam et eius conversionis[1] facere, quomodo antiquitus[2] traditur, illi fuisse premonstrata. Quod non tam condenso quomodo audivimus verbo, sed pro veritate certantes, eo quod credimus factum brevi replicamus et sensu, licet ab illis minime audivimus famatum qui eius plura pre ceteris sciebant. Nec tamen quod tam spiritaliter a fidelibus traditur, tegi silentio per totum rectum rimamur, cum etiam sepe fama cuiusque rei, per longa tempora terrarumque spatia, post congesta, diverso modo *p. 90* in aures diversorum perveniet. / Hoc igitur multo ante horum omnes qui nunc supersunt, gestum est dies. Verum itaque[3] omnes fuisse[4] scimus quia idem rex fuit exul sub rege Uuestanglorum[5] Redualdo, quem emulus suus sic passim persecutus est, qui eum ex patria pulsit tirannus[6]

---
[9] ansportatur *M1*   [10] antiq: *M1*   [11] scelum *M1*   [12] om *inserted and erased M1*
[1] conversationis *M1*   [2] antiquitur *M1*   [3] t *above M2*   [4] *ed.* fuise *M1*
[5] uuestranglorum *M1*   [6] tirannis *M1*

Gregory the Great

was to be kept until the instruction of the catechumens was finished and then brought into the hall. Then when they were all gathered together there, he gave the people of God who were recent converts and still uninstructed, a very good reason for this event; he assured them that they ought to learn from so clear a sign that that ancient evil called idolatry was in all respects useless; "for," he said, "if that senseless bird was unable to avoid death, still less could it foretell the future to men who have been reborn and baptized into the image of God, who 'have dominion over the fish of the sea and over the fowl of the air and over every living thing upon earth';[62] yet these foretellers boast that they understand the ways of birds by their own native cunning and so deceive the foolish, as God's permissive will allows."

[Chapter 16]

Since we are mentioning Edwin, our most Christian king, it would also be proper to tell of his conversion and how, according to ancient tradition, it was revealed to him beforehand. We will tell the story, not in the condensed form in which we heard it,[63] but we will seek to tell the truth and briefly relate what we believe to have happened, even though we have not heard it from those who knew him better than most. However, we do not hold it to be entirely right to hide in silence what is related so sincerely by faithful witnesses, for often the account of any event which happened long ago and in distant lands and which was put into shape in later times, reaches the ears of different people in different forms. For this happened long before the days of any of those who are still alive.[64] We all know that it is true that King Edwin was an exile at the court of Rædwald, King of the East Angles.[65] The tyrant

Ẹdilfridus, ut eum pecunia sua emere occidendum querebat. Ea tempestate dicunt ei de sua vita consternato quadam die quidam pulchrẹ visionis, cum cruce Christi coronatus apparens eum consolari coepisse, promittens ei felicem vitam regnumque gentis sue futurum, si ei obedire[7] voluisset. Eoque promittente voluisse, si verum probaret sibi quod promisit respondit, "Probabis hoc[8] verum et qui tibi primo[9] cum hac speciẹ et signo apparebit, illi debes oboedire. Qui te uni Deo qui creavit omnia, vivo et vero docebit obedire, quique Deus daturus est tibi ea que promitto et omnia quẹ tibi agenda sunt per illum demonstrabit[10]." Sub hac igitur speciẹ[11] dicunt illi Paulinum prefatum episcopum primo apparuisse.

[Chapter 17]

O piissime pater, Domine Deus omnipotens, licet predictam beati Gregorii minime mereremur presentiam, per eum tamen tibi semper sit gratiarum actio doctoris nostri Paulini, quem in fine suo fidelem tibi ostendisti. Nam fertur a videntibus quod huius viri anima in cuiusdam magne, qualis est cignus, alba specie avis, satisque pulchra, quando moritur migrasset ad cẹlum.

[Chapter 18]

Sed ut propositum persequar, qualibet Christi lucerna / de hoc rege Eduino signorum lucescit floribus dico, ut apertius merita clarescant. Huius itaque regalis vere viri ossium[1]

---

[7] oebedire *M1* [8] *above M2* [9] promo *M1* [10] demonstravit *M1* [11] *First* e *above M2* [1] *alt. from* ossarium *M1*

Æthelfrith, his rival, drove him hither and thither, seeking to bring about his death by paying out sums of money. On one occasion during this period, when he was in fear of his life, it is said that a certain man, lovely to look upon, appeared to him crowned with the cross of Christ and began to comfort him, promising him a happy life and the restoration of his kingdom if he would obey him. Edwin assured him that he would be ready to do so if he could prove to him that what he promised was true. The man answered, "You will prove it to be true and you must obey him who first appears to you in this form and with this sign. He will teach you to submit to Him the one living and true God[66] who created all things; it is He who will give you what I promise and will show you through that man all that you ought to do." It is said to have been Bishop Paulinus[67] who first appeared to him in that form.

[Chapter 17]

O most merciful Father, Lord God Almighty, though as we have seen we were not worthy to have St. Gregory with us in person, yet we continually give Thee thanks for our teacher Paulinus, who, through Gregory's agency, became our teacher. And at his last moment Thou didst show him to be faithful to Thee, because it is related by some who saw it that, when he died, his soul journeyed to heaven in the form of an exceedingly beautiful great white bird, like a swan.[68]

[Chapter 18]

But to continue our theme, I go on to describe how the light of Christ shines from this King Edwin in the glory of his miracles in order that his merits may blaze forth more brightly. So it is proper to record how the relics, con-

reliquię qualiter Domino revelante sunt reperte, dignum est memorię commendare. Fuit igitur frater quidam nostrę gentis nomine Trimma, in quodam monasterio Sudranglorum[2] presbiterii functus[3] officio,[4] diebus Edilredi regis illorum, adhuc in vita monastica vivente, Aeonfleda filia religiosi regis prefati Eduini. Cui per somnium presbitero[5] vir quidam visus est dicens ei, "Vade ad locum quem dixero tibi, qui est in regione illa que dicitur Hedfled quo Eduinus rex occisus est. Debes enim ossa eius exinde tollere tecum ad Streunesalae deducere,"[6] quod est coenobium famosissimum[7] Aelflede, filię supradicte regine[8] Eonflede natę, ut supra diximus, Eduini, femina valde iam religiosa. Cui respondit presbiter dicens, "Nescio illum locum; quomodo possum quo ignoro proficisci?" At ille, "Vade," inquit, "ad vicum illum in Lindissi[9]" (cuius nomen frater noster, illius presbiteri cognatus, qui hanc mihi exposuit ystoriam non recolebat) "et quere in eo maritum quendam nomine Teoful. Interroga illum de loco; ipse potest tibi monstrare ubi est." Presbiter itaque sciens esse somniorum

p. 92 fallatia multimoda, nimirum de qua scriptum est / multos errare[10] fecerunt somnia, dimisit rem adhuc taliter ostensa.[11] Unde post hec ab eodem viro validius admonitus, alteri e suis sicut illi monstratum est, retulit fratribus. Sed ipse eodem quo diximus modo agnoscit somnium eum fecit [12]quid esset[13] dimittere.

[*Chapter 19*]
His itaque peractis tertio adhuc vir suus eodem presbitero apparuit [1]eumque flagello satis redargutione correxit, sicque[2] increpans ait, "Nonne bis indicavi tibi quid debes

---

[2] Sundaranglorum *M2*   [3] funtus *M1*   [4] oficio *M1*   [5] s *above M2*   [6] deduere *M1*   [7] *ed.* famasisimum *M1*   [8] *ed.* regi *M1* na *above over erasure of* Aelflede *M2*   [9] *ed.* Lindis sicuius *M1*   [10] erare *M1*   [11] sic *M1*   [12-13] *ed.* quide esset *M1* quide esse *M2*   [1-2] *om. M1: ins. at bottom of page M2*

sisting of the royal man's bones, were found through the revelation of God. Now there was a certain brother of our race named Trimma who exercised the office of priest in a monastery of the South English,[69] in the days of their king Æthelred, while Eanflæd was still living and in the monastic life. She was the daughter of that same pious king, Edwin. A certain man appeared in a dream to the priest and said to him, "Go to a place that I will tell you of, in the district known as Hatfield Chase, where King Edwin was killed. You must remove his bones from there and take them to *Streoneshealh* [Whitby]." This is the well-known monastery of Ælfflæd, a most religious woman and the daughter of Queen Eanflæd, who was herself, as we have said above, the daughter of Edwin.[70] The priest answered, "I do not know the place. How can I go to a place I do not know?" But the man answered, "Go to such and such a village in Lindsey"[71] (our brother who told me the story and who was a kinsman of the priest could not remember its name) "and ask for a certain *ceorl*[72] there named Teoful. Ask him about the place and he can show you where it is." The priest, however, being well aware of the multitudinous deceptions associated with dreams—for is it not written that "dreams have caused many to err"?[73]—dismissed the matter which had so far only been revealed to him in this way. Again the priest was more sharply warned by the same man and so he related what had been revealed to him to another of the brothers. He, too, in the same way, looked upon it as a dream and made him dismiss the question of what it could mean.

[Chapter 19]

After this the man appeared for the third time to the priest; he corrected him and reproved him violently, even

facere et neglexisti? Proba³ modo si adhuc inoboediens an oboediens mihi esse volueris." Tum scilicet festinanter perrexit ad maritum prefatum; eumque ocius querendo ubi esset, invenit secundum quod illi monstratum est. A quo satis diligenter sciscitando didicit signis aperte monstratis, quo iam quęrere reliquias debuisset regis.⁴ Statimque comperto, profectus est ad locum sibi demonstratum⁵. Et primo fodiens non invenit adhuc quod querebat; sed secundo laboriosius fodiendo, ut sepe fieri solet, inventumque thesarum desiderabile ad hoc nostrum secum asportavit⁶ coenobium. In quo nunc honorifice in sancti Petri apostolorum⁷ principis ecclesia hec eadem sancta ossa cum ceteris conduntur regibus nostris ad austrum altaris illius, quod beatissimi Petri apostoli est nomine⁸ sanctificatum, et ab oriente illius quod in hac ipsa sancto Gregorio est consecrata eclesia. Fertur quoque ab hoc relatum presbitero qui postea pro tempore / prioris sanctum iamque habitavit locum sepultionis crebro se⁹ iam vidisse¹⁰ spiritus interfectorum iiii, per nimirum baptizatorum¹¹, splendide venientes sua corpora visitasse et adiecit si posset monasterium¹² ibi¹³ voluisse facere.

[*Chapter 20*]

His igitur peractis relationibus, quę proprię ad nos pertineat, adhuc ea sequamur quibus, Christo in se quoque loquente vir beatissimus Gregorius signorum est sanctitate famatus nobiscum¹. Nam antiquorum fertur esse narratio quia quędam² Romę aliquando matrona sibi oblationes

---

³ probo *M1*   ⁴ *word erased after* regis, *probably* ossarium   ⁵ de *above M2*
⁶ *ed.* asportabit *M1*   ⁷ apostorum *M1*   ⁸ nomini *M1*   ⁹ *above M2*   ¹⁰ vindicte (?) *M1*   ¹¹ *ed* baptizatatorum *M1*   ¹² manasterium *M1*   ¹³ *ed.* ubi *M1*
¹ nonicum *M1*   ² dam *above M2*

Gregory the Great 105

using a whip,[74] at the same time rebuking him with such words as these, "Have I not twice shown you what you must do and you have taken no notice? Now show me whether you intend to obey or disobey me." Then he quickly went off to look for this *ceorl* and, on making enquiries, soon found him according to the directions given him. He questioned the *ceorl* closely and learned by certain marks, which the man explained clearly, where he ought to look for the King's relics. As soon as he got the information, he went at once to the place which had been pointed out to him, but on his first dig he did not find what he was looking for; however, after digging more carefully a second time, as often happens, he found the treasure he desired and brought it with him to our monastery here. And now the holy bones are honourably buried in the Church of St. Peter,[75] the chief of the Apostles, together with other of our kings, on the south side of the altar which is dedicated in the name of the blessed Apostle Peter and east of the altar dedicated to St. Gregory, which is in the same church. It is also related by this priest who afterwards lived for a time by the holy site of the first burial that he had frequently seen the spirits of four of the slain, who were undoubtedly baptized people,[76] coming in splendid array to visit their own bodies. The priest added that, if he could have done so, he would have liked to build a monastery there.

[Chapter 20]

Having brought these stories to an end,[77] we will follow them up with some which rightly concern us, among whom St. Gregory is famous on account of his holy miracles and through whom Christ also speaks. There is an ancient story that once a certain matron in Rome was mak-

faciens, eas³ adtulisset, quas iam vir sanctus accipiens in sacrosancti corporis Christi sanctificavit agoniam. Cumque illa venisset eam communicare de manu Dei hominis atque illum audivit⁴ dicentem, "Corpus Domini nostri Iesu Christi conservet animam tuam," subrisit. Quod vir Domini videns, clausit manum suam contra os⁵ eius, et nolens ei dare sanctum corpus Domini, posuit super altare eiusque vestimento ut sibi placuit abscondit. Missa vero peracta, eam sibi advocans interrogavit⁶ cur subrideret quando communicare debuit. Illa respondens ait, "Ego ipsos panes meis feci manibus, et tu de illis dixisti quia corpus Domini essent." Tum concite secum populum Dei pariter admonuit orare in eclesia ut Christus filius Dei vivi dignaretur

p. 94 ostendere an verum corpus eius esset, ut ait, illius / sacrosanctum sacrificium ad confirmandam incredulitatem eius quę huic erat incredula sacramento. Qua peracta oratione⁷, sanctus vir invenit super altare quod posuit ut digituli auricularis particulam⁸ sanguilenti. Ad quod mirabile spectaculum vocavit incredulam, quo iam viso satis obstupuit⁹. Cui sanctus vir ait, "Nunc carnalibus considera oculis, quod prius obcecata¹⁰ celestibus minime potuisti conspicere et disce ei esse credula qui dixit, 'Nisi manducaveritis carnem filii hominis et biberitis eius sanguinem non habebitis vitam in vobis.'" Eosque iterum qui erant in eclesia hortatus est ad orationem, ut ille qui eis misericordiam suam quam postulabant ostendere dignatus est, iterum dignaretur sacrum corpus suum in suam mutare naturam, de quo eum presumebant, tantum¹¹ pro infidelitate incredule mulieris precari. Quod cum fecissent ut

---

³ *ed.* ea *M1*   ⁴ *erasure before* dicentem   ⁵ hos *M2*   ⁶ *second* i *above M1*
⁷ oratio *M1*   ⁸ parculam *M1*   ⁹ obstipuit *M1*   ¹⁰ obceca *M1*   ¹¹ *over erasure M1*

ing her oblations and had brought them to him; the saint received them and consecrated them into the most holy Body of Christ the Victim. When she came to receive it from the hands of the man of God and heard him say, "The Body of our Lord Jesus Christ preserve thy soul,"[78] she began to smile. When the man of God saw this, he closed his hand as it reached her mouth, not wishing to give her the holy Body of the Lord; then he placed it on the altar and decided to hide it with his vestment.[79] When mass was finished, he called her up and asked why she laughed when she should have communicated. She answered, "I made those loaves with my own hands and you said they were the Body of the Lord." Then he at once bade all the people of God in the church to pray together with him that Christ the Son of the living God[80] would deign to show whether the most holy sacrifice was, as he said, truly His Body in order to strengthen the faith of her who did not believe in this sacrament. When he had finished speaking, the saint found that what he had placed on the altar was like the fragment of a little finger and covered with blood. He called the unbelieving woman to behold the marvelous sight and when she saw it she was utterly dumbfounded. Then the saint said, "Now look with bodily eyes on what you were before too blind to see with your spiritual eyes and learn to believe on Him who said, "Except ye eat the flesh of the Son of Man and drink His blood, ye have no life in you."[81] He again urged those who were in church to pray that He who deigned to show them the mercy they had asked for, would also deign to change the sacred Body back into its natural form; this they ventured to pray for and also for the lack of faith of the incredulous matron. When they had done as he bade

docuit, fecit eam communicare credulam illi a quo dictum est, "Qui manducat corpus meum et bibit[12] meum sanguinem in me manet et ego in eo."

[*Chapter 21*]

Est et altera vetus quoque relatio viri Dei istius famę, in qua quidam dicuntur e partibus Romam venisse occidentalibus, missi a domino suo ut exinde sibi reliquias[1] sanctorum aliquas adferrent. Quos vir Domini Gregorius gratanter / excipiens diebus quibus ibi manserunt indesinenter missas agendo eis sanctas diversorum Dei[2] martirum reliquias[3] consecravit sicut illic aliquando [4]mos est facere.[5] Atque eas singulis inponendo buxis pannis partim dividens [6]sigillo suo[7] signavit, eosque remeare ad suum fecit dominum[8]. Qui cum reversi in via more humano quiescere quodam coepissent[9] loco, occurrit ei animo qui primus fuit illorum stulte egissę, eo quod non consideravit quid suo domino esset allaturus. Fractis ergo sigillorum inpressionibus, nihil ibi[10] invenit habere[11], nisi ut viles admodum pannorum sectiones. Sicque ad Dei virum reversi dixerunt, si tales ad dominum suum venissent, plus se morte damnatos quam ulla gratia exceptos. Quibus primo archidiaconus dicitur respondisse quod stulte satis egissent, sancta illa signacula presumentes comminuere; seque id non ausum fuisse pontifici dicere, sed[12] suasit eis proficisci[13]. Quod cum [14]se facere[15] nullomodo audere dixerunt,—putabant enim se ossa vel maius aliquid hominum visu adlaturos,—ad extremum sancto antistiti nuntiatum est. Quod ipse paciente ferens, iterum excoepit eosque[16] fecit esse in eclesia cum populo pariter ad missam. Quem ut de priori causa dixi-

---

[12] bitbit *M1* [1] requia *M1* [2] *above M2* [3] reliqua *M1* [4-5] facere mos est *M2* [6-7] *above M2* [8] domum *M1* [9] coepere *M1* [10] sibi *M1* [11] haberi *M2* [12] *in margin M2* [13] proficisse *M1* [14-15] *above M2* [16] *above M2*

Gregory the Great

them, he made her communicate, now that she believed Him who said that "he that eateth my flesh and drinketh my blood dwelleth in me and I in Him."[82]

[Chapter 21]

There is also another ancient tradition about this famous man of God which tells how some men came to Rome from western parts, having been sent by their master to bring him some relics of the saints from that city.[83] Gregory, the man of God, received them gladly and during the days they remained in Rome consecrated some holy relics of various martyrs by constantly celebrating holy masses for them as the custom once was. Then he divided up the pieces of cloth, putting them into separate boxes and sealing them with his seal; so he sent the men back to their master. On their return journey, while they were resting by the wayside as men do, it occurred to their leader that he had done foolishly in not finding out what he was taking back to his master. So he broke the impressions of the seals and found nothing inside the boxes except just some dirty pieces of cloth. Thereupon they returned to the man of God, saying that if such rags came to their master, they were more likely to be condemned to death than to be received with any thanks. First of all, the archdeacon is said to have told them that they had acted very foolishly in presuming to break those sacred seals; he added that he did not dare to tell the Pope but urged them to go back again. They answered that they could not possibly venture to return, for they had believed that they were taking back bones or at least something more important in the sight of men than rags. So at last the Holy Father was told. He was very patient with them, received them back again, and bade them be in church at mass with the rest of the people.

mus¹⁷ Deum ortatus est deprecari ostendere¹⁸ suorum an vere essent sanctorum reliquię martyrum quas illis donavit
p. 96 legatis. / Cum autem¹⁹ esset²⁰ oratum ab omnibus, tulit ipse cultellum²¹ quem sibi iussit donare et unum e pannis pungendo secavit, ex quo confestim sanguis secto cucurrit. Itaque dixit ad eos, "Nescitis quod in sanctificatione corporis et sanguinis Christi, cum supra sancta eius altaria ei in libamen ob sanctificationem illorum offerebantur reliquiarum, sanguis²² sanctorum quibus adsignata est semper illos intravit pannos utique tinctos?" Qui cum hec viderunt et audierunt, satis consternati, cum²³ omnibus admirabantur quę viderunt et audierunt. Ubi statim ut supra per orationem Deum dixit²⁴ orandum ut fides²⁵ esset²⁶ adfirmanda. Quo scilicet effecto²⁷ reversi, domino suo nuntiabant hec universa. Que ipse audiens tam sancti viri auditis oraculis quam fide divina de qua scriptum est, "Omne quod non est ex fide peccatum est,"²⁸ eam mundo corde adcommodavit omnibus de his que audivit, credens ei²⁹ de quo dicitur, "Mundans fide corda eorum." Unde etiam maiora quam in sancti Petri eclesia inibi dicuntur sepe efulsisse miracula. O mirabilis Deus in sanctis suis; Deus Israel ipse dabit virtutem et fortitudinem plebi suę. Benedictus Deus!

[*Chapter 22*]

Tertia ad hęc sequitur eius opinio celebritatis, in qua illum secutus est, qui unus in trina deitate non est personarum /
p. 97 acceptor Deus. Sed in omni gente qui timet eum et operatur iustitiam, acceptus est illi. Fuit ergo vir quidam Romę,

---

¹⁷ *twice, second time crossed out MS*   ¹⁸ *re above M2*   ¹⁹ *above M2*   ²⁰ autem *erased M1*   ²¹ *erasure between* cul *and* tellum *M1*   ²² sangus *M1*   ²³ com *M1*   ²⁴ dux *M1*   ²⁵ ed. tales *M1*   ²⁶ *above M2*   ²⁷ affectu *M1*   ²⁸ *insert M2*   ²⁹ *insert M2*

Then, as happened in our former story, he urged the people to pray to God to show them whether what he had given the messengers were authentic relics of the holy martyrs. After they had all prayed, he told them to give him a knife which he took and with it made an incision into one of the pieces of cloth, whereupon blood at once ran from the cut. Thereupon he said to them, "Do you not know that at the consecration of the Body and Blood of Christ, when the relics are placed on His holy altar as an offering to sanctify them, the blood of the saints to whom each relic belongs always enters into the cloth just as if it had been soaked in blood?" They were greatly perturbed and amazed at what they had seen and heard and so were all the onlookers. Whereupon, as in the previous story, he said that they must seek God in prayer so that their faith might be strengthened. When this was done they returned home and told their master all these things. When he heard their story he was moved by what Gregory had said and also by holy faith, of which it is written that "whatsoever is not of faith is sin." He accepted with a pure heart what he had heard concerning all these relics, believing Him who is said to "purify their hearts by faith."[84] And so even greater miracles are said to have shone forth more frequently from their new resting-place than in the Church of St. Peter itself. "O how marvelous is God in his saints; the God of Israel is He who shall give strength and power unto His people. Blessed be God."[85]

[Chapter 22]

Still further there is a third instance of his renown, in which Gregory followed Him, the One in Three who is "no accepter of persons but in every nation he that feareth Him and worketh righteousness is accepted with Him."[86]

dives in rebus sed egenus in religione, cui cum uxor sua displicuit, fecit sibi ab ea, contra preceptum Domini salvatoris nostri, divortium. Cui continuo pontifex summus sanctus Gregorius non adquievit carni et sanguini, sed ei cito in nomine Domini Iesu Christi obnisus eius mandatum prevaricanti resistit. Eumque fiducialiter, quem edocere[1] leniter noluit, excommunicavit. Quam excommunicationis sententiam non facile ferens, sua adhuc augendo scelera, magorum quęsivit adiumenta duorum, quibus pecuniam promittendo placabilem, illi fecit eos insidiasse. Tum eum nescientes quodam eminenti loco quadam die stare coeperunt. Cum idem vir Dei ad quandam missarum profectus est sollemnitatem, tunc illum[2] sciscitantes quis esset, a quodam didicerunt solum equitem[3] post cuneum et clerum precedentem vel subsequentem. Quem cum viderunt arte sua demonia excitantes, miserunt ut ei mali aliquid fecissent. Statimque hostes magni equum eius intrantes quem sedebat, cito insanire fecerunt. Quod vir sanctus videns consueta contra eos, iuxta apostolum, adsumendo armaturam Dei, primum crucis Christi signaculum hostilem ocius effugavit / insaniam. Statim quoque circa se quid esset diligentius intuendo, vidit ipsos magos imę mentis eminus stantes altius a ceteris. Quos incircumscriptus Spiritus sanctus perpetua cito sic cecitate percussit, ut cadentes deorsum conlapsi sunt crudeliter, qui se inmundo replentes spiritu ab eo prius reciderunt; cuius confestim

---

[1] re *above M2*   [2] *above M2*   [3] equitatem *M1*

Gregory the Great

There was a man in Rome who was rich in possessions but poor in piety;[87] when his wife displeased him he obtained a divorce from her, contrary to the teaching of our Lord and Saviour. Thereupon Pope St. Gregory "conferred not with flesh and blood,"[88] but forthwith opposed him in the name of the Lord Jesus Christ and resisted him when he disobeyed his command; then, when he could not teach him by gentler means, he boldly excommunicated him. The man did not take the sentence of excommunication easily but even increased his wrongdoing by seeking the help of two magicians, whom he persuaded to plot against Gregory by promising them enough money to satisfy them. They did not know him, but on a certain day they took up their position on a high place.[89] Then, when the man of God was on his way to celebrate a solemn mass, they enquired which one was Gregory and were told that he rode alone on a horse after the crowds, either behind or in front of the body of clergy. As soon as they saw him they began to arouse their devils by their arts and sent them to do him some evil. Forthwith the powerful foes entered the horse he was riding and quickly maddened it. When the saint saw it, in the words of the Apostle, he "took the whole armour of God"[90] against them as was his custom and the very first time he made the sign of the cross of Christ he forthwith banished the frenzy of the enemy. At the same time he looked round carefully to see what the matter was and caught sight of these hellish-minded magicians standing apart and higher than the others. The Holy Spirit that knows no bounds forthwith struck them with perpetual blindness, so that they both collapsed and fell to the ground in a frightful manner; they had previously rejected the Holy Spirit and been filled

dono sanctus vir Gregorius inluminatus agnovit eos videndo conruentes sibi fuisse adducendos. Quos coram se cum essent, inquisivit de causa; qui ei dixerunt virum illum prefatum ab eis per pecuniam inpetrasse ut ei in ultionem sui facerent malum quodcumque potuissent. Quibus ipse ait, "Ceci esse debetis in perpetuum, quia si lumen oculorum vestrorum habebitis, iterum reverti volueritis ad artem vestram pessimam eamque per demones ut prius excolere." Hac igitur ex causa postremo dicuntur ad Deum conversi, Christi baptismate consepulti. Eosque tales vir Domini sanctus Gregorius ecclesiastica[4] stipe quamdiu viverent[5], mandavit, alendos pauperes, perfectos pro Domino medicos animarum.

[*Chapter 23*]

Inter hec neque illud signum sapientię et gratię Dei in eo silendum est, licet ex parte, ut cetera, nesciatur ex nobis; nam et inter multa gesta illius mirifica, in quibus maxime peritię medicus fuit animarum, fertur scilicet tali signo effulsisse et[1] corporum. Fuit igitur rex quidam, quem puto Langobardorum fuisse, qui non evidenter cuius esset gentis re/miniscor, qui illius pontificatus tempore bellipotens, exercitum suum[2] contra Romam depopulare eam cogitando, duxit.[3] Cui sanctus vir Gregorius obviam factus, eumque in praesentia eorum[4] adlocutus, eius fervidum pectus singularis in se doctrinę divinę sic molle[5] fecit affluentia, ut promisit ei quamdiu ipse esset pontifex in illa urbe numquam gens sua, eo regnante, exercitum duceret contra eum. Sicque per Dei[6] virum illius fluminis impetus letifi-

---

[4] ti *above* M2   [5] viverunt M1   [1] *above* M2   [2] sum M1   [3] *ed. omit* MS
[4] *ed.* rum M1   [5] *ed.* male M1   [6] *above* M2

Gregory the Great 115

with an unholy spirit. Gregory, who was illuminated by the gift of the same Holy Spirit, recognized, as he saw them tumbling in a heap, that they had been brought together to do him harm. So when they were summoned into his presence, he enquired the cause. They told him that the man we have spoken of had bribed them to do Gregory whatever evil they could, out of revenge. He said, "You must remain blind forever because, if you had your sight, you would desire to return to your evil arts and practise them as before, with the help of the devils." For this reason it is said that they were finally converted to God and buried with Christ in baptism.[91] St. Gregory, the man of God, so long as they lived, entrusted them with the church funds for caring for the poor, so that they became righteous healers of souls for the Lord.[92]

[Chapter 23]

Among these anecdotes we must not fail to tell this sign of the wisdom and grace of God, even though, as in the rest of these stories, we do not know the full details; amid the many marvelous things he did in which he showed himself to be an exceedingly skilful doctor of souls,[93] it is told how, by a like miracle, he shone forth also as a doctor of the body. Now there was a certain king, I think a king of the Lombards,[94] though I do not clearly remember his race, who was very powerful in war when Gregory was Pope; he marched his army against Rome intending to devastate it. St. Gregory went to meet him and spoke to him before them all and thus, by his unique eloquence and holy instruction, so mollified the King's frenzied spirit that he promised so long as Gregory was Pope in that city and he was King, his nation would never lead an army against them. So, through the agency of the man of God, "The

cavit civitatem Dei qua scilicet in eo sanctificavit[7] Deus tabernaculum suum et adiuvabit eum Deus vultu suo, ut conturbate gentes contra olim dominam orbis per unum hominem Dei[8] inclinata sunt regna. Nec inmerito: per quem dedit vocem suam altissimus et mota est terra. Hic igitur rex post hęc egrotavit et misit ad sanctum pontificem prefatum pro sua infirmitate: qui illum sibi magistrum ex predicta eius elegit doctrina. Cui protinus per[9] nuntios audita mandavit infirmitate ut ad illum redisset cybum, quo puerulus adhuc[10] atque infantulus vescebatur. Ergo rex iste, cum puer esset, fuit intra Alpes cum pastoribus peccorum et erat lacteo nutritus cybo. Ad quem, secundum viri Dei[11] doctrinam rediens, continuo melius habere coepit. Hęc igitur sensu in quibusdam proferimus, ne ut ipse de sanctorum ait actibus quę scripsit, rustice dicentes nil spiritale dicamus. /

[*Chapter 24*]

p. 100 Huius denique verius inter cetera viri signum sanctitatis, quod maius est mirandum, omnibus quod in scriptis suis tam preclarum inluxit illi cęleste in se Christo, ut prediximus, loquente ingenium, sicut in omeliis eius est omnibus conspicuum considerantibus, de quo ipse, "Predicate," ait, "evangelium omni creaturę." Quod tam plene tamque ab eo suscipit sapienter, qui est Dei sapientia in mysterio abscondita, quem predestinavit[1] Deus ante secula in gloriam nostram, ut a gente Romana quę pre ceteris mundo intonat sublimius[2] proprię[3] de aurea oris eius gratia, os[4]

---

[7] *ed.* letificavit *M1*   [8] *above M2*   [9] inter *erased MS*   [10] *above M2*   [11] Deo *M1*   [1] *ed.* predistinavit *M1*   [2] *second* i *above M2*   [3] *sic MS*   [4] s *above M2*

streams of that river made glad the city of God" and in it "He sanctified His tabernacle." God did indeed "help her with His countenance"; so that though "the heathen raged" against the city that was once the mistress of the world, yet through this one man of God the "kingdoms were moved." And not without reason, for "the most High uttered His voice and the earth trembled."[95] Now after this the King was taken ill and in his sickness sent to the Pope; for as a result of Gregory's teaching he had taken the Pope as his mentor. Thereupon when he had learned all about the King's illness from the messengers he ordered that the King should return to the kind of food he had been used to from his infancy and childhood. Now when the King was a boy he had been in the Alps with herdsmen and lived on milky foods. So, in accordance with the instructions of the man of God, he returned to this kind of food and continued to make improvement. In some of these stories we give the sense only, lest, as he himself says, concerning the acts of the saints in the book which he wrote, by quoting their rustic speech we might fail to utter spiritual truths.[96]

[Chapter 24]

Among other signs of this man's holiness, one very true and wholly admirable sign is that in all his writings there shone forth an outstanding heavenly skill, for, as we have already said, Christ spoke through him. This is clear to all who study his *Homilies*.[97] It is Christ Himself who says, "Preach the gospel to every creature." Gregory inherited this abundant skill as well as his wisdom from Him who is the "wisdom of God in a mystery, even the hidden wisdom which God ordained before the world unto our glory":[98] therefore he was called the "golden-mouthed"[99]

aureum appellatur. De quo pulchrę[5] Dei loquitur sapientia dicens[6], "Thesaurus desiderabilis requiescit in ore sapientis," que bene ad eum dirigitur, id quod de Christo legitur dictum, "Diffusa est gratia in labiis tuis," quod non solum per illum hominis filium, sed per eius quoque membra completur. Quod per hunc virum Domini voce velut[7] viva usque hodie suavitate resonat nobis melliflua. "Interpretabor," ait sanctus Hieronimus[8], "in menbris quod fertur ad caput": intellegam de servis quod impleatur in domino, quia gloria domini gloria famulorum sit. Et ubicumque oportunitas loci se obtulerit, sic de vero lumine disputabo ut dirivetur ad eos quibus Christus donavit ut lumen sint. De quo cum dixit[9], "Vos estis lux mundi," et postea omnibus / lucere in domo debere ostendit. Necnon et ait, "Luceat lux vestra coram hominibus" et reliqua: ecce etiam in hoc[10] viro non tam coram hominibus sed etiam coram angelis lucere monstravit.

[*Chapter 25*]
Unde de ordinibus illorum, scilicet agminum[1] tali tractavit ingenio, quali nequaquam sanctorum aliquis vel ante vel post eum invenimus fecisse alterum. De quibus etiam fide integer et vita purus sanctus Augustinus, e cuius in orbem flumina ventre fluent aquę vivę, "Ego me," inquit, "ignorare ista confiteor." Hic vero eos non solum in suis distinxit[2] agminibus, omnia ex sanctis confirmando scripturis,

---
[5] *sic* MS   [6] c *above* M2   [7] velud M2   [8] Heronimus M1   [9] *above* M2
[10] *above* M2   [1] agminis M1   [2] n *above* M2

by the Romans because of the golden eloquence which issued from his mouth in a very special way, far more sublimely and beyond all others in the world. Of this gift the Wisdom of God speaks beautifully in these words, "In the mouth of the wise man there rests a treasure to be desired," so that that which was said of Christ, "Grace is poured into thy lips,"[100] applies fittingly to him, since the saying is fulfilled not only in the Son of Man himself but also through the members of His body. So through this man of God as through a living voice, the echoes of his mellifluous sweetness still resound among us today. "I shall recognize in the limbs," says St. Jerome,[101] "the qualities which are attributed to the head: I shall understand from the servants what is manifested in the Lord; because the glory of the Lord should be the glory of His servants; and this I will declare of the true light that, wherever a suitable place is found for it, it is distributed to those whom Christ has granted to be a light too." Christ was speaking of this light when he said, "Ye are the light of the world," and He afterwards explains that it ought to shine for "all who are in the house." Furthermore he says, "Let your light so shine before men," and so on[102]; but through Gregory he showed that his light shone not only before men but before angels too.

[Chapter 25]

Now Gregory dealt with the orders of the angelic ranks[103] with such skill as we have never been able to find in any other saint before or since. St. Augustine, a man sound in faith and pure of life, "out of whose belly flow rivers of living water,"[104] says, "I confess that I know nothing about these matters."[105] Not only did Gregory divide them into orders, basing everything on the Holy Scrip-

verum etiam ad nostrę consortia vitę, mundo corde quo beati tantum Deum videbunt, dirivavit. Iste igitur ille de quo ait Salvator, "Omnis scriba doctus in regno cęlorum similis est homini patrifamilias, qui profert de thesauro suo nova et vetera." Unde cum hec nova diximus in modico et vetera similiter dicenda quo thesaurus eius esse clareat cęlestis[3] sibique[4] apertus patuisse ubi neque erugo neque tinea demolitur et fures non effodiunt nec furantur.

[Chapter 26]

Nam in homeliis sancti Ezechielis prophetę, cui iam similiter celi aperti sunt, hoc idem de illo patet cito legentibus, ubi de quattuor illud animalybus tractat, quod cum fieret vox supra firmamentum, stabant et submittebant alas suas; "possunt enim" inquit, "firmamenti nomine celestes potestates[1] intellegi. Et potest firmamentum nominari unigenitus incarnatus / per hoc quod in eum nostra[2] natura ad eternitatem firmata[3] est." Congruę itaque aliquando celos, aliquando vero celum, nomine solius firmamenti intellegimus, de quo nunc signum fideliter narratum huic nostro papę cęlos aperirę testamur, quo eum Christum Dominum, sui in signum exempli gratia cęlesti monstrasse. De qua super eos scriptum est corpore quo ille in filio hominis unigenitus Patris, per virginem Spiritu sancto superveniente factus nasci dignatus est, aqua[4] a Iohanne[5] baptizato, aperti sunt ei celi et vidit, inquit, Spiritum Dei descendentem sicut columbam et venientem super se. Ita super hunc

---

[3] cęlestes *M1* [4] sibi quae *M1* [1] potes *M1* [2] *ed.* nostram *M1* [3] firmita *M1* [4] *ed.* aq: *M1* [5] Iohannoe *M1*

tures, but also, with that pure heart whereby the blessed alone shall see God, he even brought them into fellowship with this life of ours. It is he therefore of whom the Saviour says, "Every scribe which is instructed unto the Kingdom of Heaven is like unto a man that is an householder which bringeth forth out of his treasure things new and old." We have briefly mentioned these new things, and there are old things too that could be spoken of wherein his heavenly treasure shines forth and was openly revealed to him "where neither moth nor rust doth corrupt and where thieves do not break through nor steal."[106]

[Chapter 26]

In his homilies on the holy prophet Ezekiel, to whom the heavens were similarly opened up, it is at once clear to readers, in the passage where he is dealing with the four living creatures, that when there was a voice from the firmament that was over their heads, they stood and let down their wings.[107] By the firmament, he says, are to be understood the heavenly powers. And the incarnate, only-begotten Son can be called the firmament in that in Him our nature was made firm for all time. So, quite rightly, we understand that the singular noun "firmament" sometimes means "heaven" and sometimes "the heavens."[108] In this connection we now bear witness to the true story of a miracle when the heavens were opened to our Pope in the same way in which the Lord revealed Christ through heavenly grace in a miracle of a similar type. So we read that when John baptized with water the body in which the only-begotten of the Father deigned to be born of a virgin when the Holy Spirit came upon her, the heavens were opened and John saw "the Spirit of God descending like a dove and lighting upon him."[109] So it is said that a

virum Dei vidisse quidam dicitur de suis satis[6] ei familiaris, albam sedisse columbam, cum in predictum Ezechielem fecit omelias. Cui scilicet videnti valde[7] pro illo iratus accessu precepit ne quandiu ipse viveret in carne, id alicui indicaret, ne scilicet aperto celestis signo claritatis, fama extolli foris videretur humana. Unde a dextris per gloriam incedens, fecit sibi sanctorum omnium ipse quoque exemplo a sinistris gradiendi ignobilitatem.

[*Chapter 27*]

Nota quomodo hoc pulchrę priori convenit lectioni de qua diximus evangelicę. Huic namque prophetę celis[1] apertis quadriga Domini et vera cerubin scientię plenitudo[2] de filio hominis visa est. In cuiusquam[3] et ipse quoque pulchrę prefiguratione filius hominis sepe vocatur. Quis igitur dubitet et huic celos pape[4] nostro apertos, quorum ille clavicularios sibi aperire cum Petro potentiam habuit, cum et / ipse omnes quoque scale meminerit, de qua longe prediximus, vigiliorum divinorum. Quis et hoc in eo sane mentis non agnoscat, cum illa xxxii consideret volumina, quę beatum Iob exponendo, dictis Moralibus, in languentium direxit mirabile morum, contra vitia humanorum medicamina animarum. Quem ipse, de celis lumbis accinctum Dominus de suis operibus profundissimis interrogatus est; de quo, "Hoc," inquit, "divinę providentię fuit, ut percussum Iob

---

[6] actis *M1*   [7] vade *M1*   [1] celestis *M1*   [2] *ed.* multitudo (*see p.. 158n*113) *M1*
[3] quam *above M2*   [4] *ed.* papa *M1*

Gregory the Great

certain member of Gregory's household who was very intimate with him saw a white dove[110] resting upon the man of God while he was engaged in writing these homilies on Ezekiel. Gregory was very angry with him because he had approached him and seen it;[111] he instructed the man never to make this known to anyone during his lifetime, for fear that, through this clear sign of his renown in heaven, his earthly renown might be spread abroad. So, though he walked on the right hand in his glory, he was willing, like all the saints, to bring humiliation upon himself by walking on the left.[112]

[Chapter 27]

Notice how beautifully all this agrees with the Gospel passage already referred to. When the heavens were opened, the chariot of the Lord appeared to Ezekiel, and the cherubim, signifying the true fullness of knowledge,[113] were seen by the son of man. By a kind of beautiful prefiguration, Ezekiel is also often called the son of man. So who will doubt that the heavens were opened to this Pope of ours? He, together with Peter, had the power of opening the locks of these heavens, especially since he was also mindful of those beings who served as holy guardians of Jacob's ladder of which we spoke some time ago.[114] And who will fail to see in him the signs of a healthy mind if he considers the thirty-two volumes which, while he was expounding the story of the blessed Job in his *Moralia,* he directed in a marvelous manner against the vices of the human soul, offering a medicine for ailing morals? Job girded up his loins, and the Lord Himself from heaven asked him questions about His most profound works.[115] Gregory himself said, "It was the will of divine Providence that, being stricken myself, I should comment upon stricken Job,

percussus exponerem et flagellati mentem melius per flagella sentirem."

[*Chapter 28*]

Quis in eo quoque apostolicam non stupeat tantam ligandi solvendique gratiam, non solum viventes sed etiam morientes atque sub divino infernali examinę¹ constitutos, quod ad nostram adhuc viventes relegamus² utilitatem. In scriptis quoque eius hystoricis de exitu animarum multa narravit³ miracula. Nam ⁴pro occultis⁵ tribus contra sui regulam monasterii solidis, quę morientem medicum adhuc in terra immo ligavit in inferno. Quo magnum terribiliter incussit viventibus terrorem ędificationis eumque misericorditer postea ac potenter, quia porte eius non prevalebunt adversus eum, eius ex eo solvit sacrificio, qui fuit inter mortuos liber, quo se fuisse per se solutum die trigesimo⁶ ostendit in celo. Tale quid etiam celestis eius sensit in eo papa animus quod horret dicere, qui candelabri, non solum / Romanorum sed etiam totius mundi, lucerna Romę quę urbium caput est orbisque domina, sancti Heronimi lugubri ex ea emigrando infidelitate lectionis, quę Dei lampadem singulari ab eo lumine accensum, quantum⁷ in se fuit extinguens, suam idcirco merito a sancto Gregorio meruit obscurari lampadem. Nec inmerito; quia in eo lectionis quoque divine lampas hoc lucissime agendum dilu-

---

¹ *sic* MS ² religamus *M1* ³ naravit *M1* ⁴⁻⁵ occultis pro *M1* ⁶ *ed.* trigisimo *M1* ⁷ qantum *M1*

and through my scourging I should better understand the feelings of a man who had been scourged himself."[116]

[Chapter 28]

Who will not be amazed at the apostolic grace he possessed of binding and loosing not only the living but also the dying and those who by divine permission were consigned to the hosts of hell? So let us who are still alive read about this again for our own good. In his historical works he has also told of many miracles about departing souls. Thus he bound in hell a dying physician,[117] though he was still alive, because of three coins that the man had hidden away, contrary to the rule of his monastery.[118] By doing so, Gregory struck those who were still alive with a great and terrible dread, to their edification. Afterwards he had pity on the physician and because the gates of hell did not prevail against him, Gregory used his great power to free him from hell, through the sacrifice of Him who was "free among the dead."[119] So, on the thirtieth day, he showed the other monks the man who had been loosed through his efforts, now in heaven. Something of the same sort his heavenly spirit perceived in the matter of a certain Pope, a story which is dreadful to tell. Jerome was a light upon the lampstand in Rome, not only for the Romans but for the whole world; for Rome is the chief of cities and mistress of the world. So when St. Jerome left Rome through the wretched faithlessness of the Pope's judgment, that same Pope, so far as he was able, extinguished the lamp which God had lit with a light of surpassing brilliance. Therefore the Pope rightly merited that his own light should be put out by St. Gregory and not undeservedly, because the light of divine judgment which burned in Gregory made it crystal clear that it was his duty to do

cidavit.[8] Necnon et aliud simile huic testatur horribile de illo, qui fuit ipsius successor. Qui cum presul post eum Romę constituitur, famę illius quia laudem habere nequivit ei invidisse ita pronuntiatus. Cum enim sanctus vir Gregorius Christi sic caritate constringitur ut plures e populo post suam conversos susceperat[9] doctrinamque suorum, eorum non[10] facile iste ab eo secundus portavit multitudinem, dicens, "Licet Gregorius omnem potuisset excipere populum, non tamen nos omnes possumus cybare sustinereque," quod certum tertio ob prefatam maxime invidiam, dixisse narratur. Totidem quoque vicibus quibus hec illis dicebat,[11] qui eum frequentius pulsabant pro necessitatibus predictorum a sancto Gregorio adsumptorum ei apparuisse, non leniter adlocutus dicitur cur ista de se sic iudicasset in eo quod tantum pro Domino faciebat.[12] Cumque eius[13] non adquievit sermonibus, tertia vice eum adloquens, pede suo percussit in caput. Cuius dolore percussionis in paucis diebus / defunctus est.

[Chapter 29]

Quidam quoque de nostris dicunt narratum a Romanis, sancti Gregorii lacrimis animam Traiani imperatoris refrigeratam vel baptizatam, quod est dictu mirabile et auditu. Quod autem eum dicimus babtizatum, neminem moveat: nemo enim sine babtismo Deum videbit umquam: cuius tertium genus[1] est[2] lacrimę. Nam die quadam transiens per forum Traianum, quod ab eo opere mirifico constructum dicunt, illud considerans repperit opus tam elemosinarium eum fecisse paganum ut Christiani plus

---

[8] delucidavit M1   [9] susciperat M1   [10] above M2   [11] decebat M1   [12] feciebat M1   [13] above M2   [1] over erasure M2   [2] above M2

this.[120] Another terrifying story[121] similar to this is told of the Pope who was Gregory's successor, for when he was consecrated to the papacy after Gregory at Rome, he is said to have been jealous of Gregory's fame because he could not win the praise that his predecessor won. For the latter was so constrained by the love of Christ that he made provision for many of the populace who had been converted by his teaching and by that of his people; but his successor was not ready to provide for such a multitude and said, "Even though Gregory could take care of all these people, yet we cannot feed and keep them all," and he is said to have made this statement on at least three occasions, mostly out of envy. Each time he said it to those who very frequently urged upon him their need of such provisions as they had received from St. Gregory, the saint appeared to him and is said to have asked him in far from gentle tones why he had judged his motives so wrongly when he had done it for the Lord's sake alone. Since Gregory was unable to silence him by his words, on the third occasion he kicked the man on the head. His successor died in a few days from the pain of the blow.

[Chapter 29]

Some of our people also tell a story related by the Romans[122] of how the soul of the Emperor Trajan was refreshed and even baptized by St. Gregory's tears, a story marvelous to tell and marvelous to hear. Let no one be surprised that we say he was baptized, for without baptism none will ever see God; and a third kind of baptism is by tears.[123] One day as he was crossing the Forum,[124] a magnificent piece of work for which Trajan is said to have been responsible, he found on examining it carefully that Trajan, though a pagan, had done a deed so charitable that

quam pagani esse posse videret.³ Fertur namque contra hostes exercitum ducens propere pugnaturus, unius ad eum voce viduę misericorditer mollitus, substetisse totius imperator orbis. Ait enim illa, "Domne Traiane, hic sunt homines qui filium meum occiderunt, nolentes mihi rationem reddere." Cui, "Cum rediero," inquit, "dicito mihi et faciam eos tibi rationem reddere." At illa, "Domine," ait, "si inde non venies, nemo me adiuvet." Tunc iam concite reos in eam fecit coram se in armis suis subarratam ei pecuniam conponere quam⁴ debuerunt. Hoc igitur sanctus inveniens Gregorius, id esse agnovit quod legimus, "Iudicate pupillo et defendite viduam et venite et arguite me, dicit Dominus." Unde per eum in se habuit Christum loquentem ad refrigerium animę eius quid implendo nesciebat, ingrediens ad sanctum Petrum solita direxit lacrimarum / fluenta usque dum promeruit sibi divinitus revelatum fuisse exauditum⁵, atque ut numquam de altero illud presumpsisset pagano.

[*Chapter 30*]

His igitur omnibus almi huius viri signis utcumque de gestis eorum, in Christo obsecramus lectorem, si quid melius scire possit in illis ne vituperationis sę dente nostrę adrodet opus diligentię tanti viri dilectione magis quam scientia extorsum, de qua ipse scripsit quod legitur, "Fortis est ut mors¹ dilectio"; ne forte melius fructum facere prevalendo nolens, ipsius Christi securem sibi ad conburendum se, in crura exciso radicitus convertat. Caritas enim urget nos iuxta nostri modulum ingenioli hoc memorie tradere

---

³ videtur (?) M1 ⁴ quem M1 ⁵ ed. exauditus *with* s *expunged* M1 ¹ s *above* M2

Gregory the Great

it seemed more likely to have been the deed of a Christian than of a pagan. For it is related that, as he was leading his army in great haste against the enemy, he was moved to pity by the words of a widow, and the emperor of the whole world came to a halt. She said, "Lord Trajan, here are the men who killed my son and are unwilling to pay me recompense."[125] He answered, "Tell me about it when I return and I will make them recompense you." But she replied, "Lord, if you never return, there will be no one to help me." Then, armed as he was, he made the defendants pay forthwith the compensation they owed her, in his presence. When Gregory discovered this story, he recognized that this was just what we read about in the Bible, "Judge the fatherless, plead for the widow. Come now and let us reason together, saith the Lord."[126] Since Gregory did not know what to do to comfort the soul of this man who brought the words of Christ to his mind, he went to St. Peter's Church and wept floods of tears, as was his custom, until he gained at last by divine revelation the assurance that his prayers were answered, seeing that he had never presumed to ask this for any other pagan.

[Chapter 30]

So if any reader should know more about all the miracles of this kindly man or how they happened, we pray him, for Christ's sake, not to nibble with critical teeth at this work of ours which has been diligently twisted into shape by love rather than knowledge, a love of which it is written that "love is strong as death." It may be that if such a reader is unwilling by his own efforts to produce better fruit, he may even turn the axe of Christ upon himself so that he is cut down root and branch to be burned. For "the love of Christ constraineth us" to preserve the memory of

signa, de hoc nostro Deo nobis donante doctore. Unde etiam, quia semper est pro veritate certandum catholica, quantum in nobis est verum diximus. Id vero scrupulum nec ulli moveat, licet horum ordo preposterus, quia id sole clarius iubar sancte scripture et sanctorum sepe auctorum in se narratio rerum rite[2] motarum demonstrat: sicuti est illud maxime auctoritatis evangelicę quod sanctus Matheus prope finem [3]sui posuit[4] libri Iesum templum intrantem et ex eo vendentes et ementes iecit[5]; quod beatus Iohannes pene posuit in sui principio voluminis; verba quoque ab eis alia pro aliis sepe posita, sensum tantum eundem. Verum iam defendunt ut est illud quod alter evangelista ovem perditam ait in montibus, alter vero in deserto, cum

p. 107 utique aliud illorum ait verborum quia[6] eam / [7]pastor in humeris Christus inventam revehit ad gregem. Sed neque et illud moveat quemquam si quid horum de alio quolibet sanctorum fuisset effectum, cum sanctus apostolus per mysterium unius corporis membrorum, sanctorum scilicet vitam conparando concordat ut simus ad invicem alter alterius membra. Fitque officium, verbi gratia, oculorum et aurium, manibus ac pedibus, sic profuturum sicut illis in commune, et ita omnia in omnibus licet non eundem actum[8] habent[9]. Inde etiam scimus sanctorum esse omnia per caritatem corporis Christi, cuius sunt membra communia. Unde si quid horum quę scripsimus de hoc viro non fuit, quae etiam non ab illis qui viderunt et audierunt per ore

---

[2] rete *M1* [3-4] pusuit suit *M1* [5] iecit *M1* [6] qui *M1* [7] *a new hand begins here, using lighter ink* [8] actuum *M3* [9] *ed.* habeant *M3*

Gregory the Great

his miracles according to this the measure of our feeble wit, and our God will provide us with instruction in this matter.[127] So because we must always strive for universal truth, we have told the truth so far as in us lies. Therefore let no one be disturbed even though the arrangement of the stories is confused, because the radiant Holy Scriptures, though brighter than the sun, and the narratives of the various holy authors often reveal in their contents such rearrangement of the subject matter as is suitable. Indeed this method finds very strong authority in the Gospels. Thus St. Matthew has placed at the end of his book the story of Jesus entering the temple and throwing out those who bought and sold, while St. John put it right at the beginning of his Gospel. Again, some words are often replaced by others, though the sense is the same. The two Evangelists are telling the truth even if one says that the sheep was lost in the mountains and the other in the wilderness;[128] at any rate each of these statements adds that Christ the shepherd found it and carried it back on his shoulders to the flock. So let no one be disturbed even if these miracles were performed by any other of the saints,[129] since the holy Apostle, through the mystery of the limbs of a single body, which he compares to the living experience of the saints, concludes that we are all "members one of another." For instance, the work of the eyes and ears becomes profitable to the hands and the feet as if they were for common use, and so all things are profitable to all even though they "have not the same office." Hence we know too that all saints have everything in common through the love of Christ of whose body they are members. Hence if anything we have written did not concern this man—and, remember, we did not learn about them directly from those

didicimus, vulgata tantum habemus, de illo eius etiam esse in magno dubitamus minime, quod iam hic sanctus vir, in sua pręfata sapientia, satis evidenter docet[10], ut amantium semper in alterutrum fiat quod cernitur in aliis. Et hoc iam in supra illa societate angelorum esse nihilominus[11], quorum ut prediximus rimatus est archana, declarat dicens quia non minus unumquemque reficit quod in altero videt quam quod in semetipso possidet. Et ut altiora repetam, Dominus Deus omnipotens sanctorum angelorum et hominum, postquam creavit omnia, per eos quos fecit ad imaginem suam, semper sua maxima ostendit miracula. Primo enim ea angeli hominibus nuntiabant optimisque illi post ea minoribus, sicut in Moysi et populo Iudeorum legimus, ceterisque sanctis usque in[12] adventum Salvatoris nostri, cuius tantum erat et est semper, salvare quod perierat; unde creavit in primordio cum in fine restauravit[13] perditum. Ostendit suam[14] et in hoc caritatem illis quibus /

p. 108 dixit, "Sicut dilexit me pater et ego dilexi vos," dans ipsis a suis maiora fecisse miracula dicens, "Maiora horum facietis." Quod sane et in doctrina potest quoque cognosci, quia indubitanter maiorem sibi Christus per suos adquisivit non solum apostolos, sed etiam et alios doctores, credentium multitudinem. Hanc[15] quoque caritatem et in futuro[16] ostendet iudicio, ubi peccatores a iustis iudicentur, quando ut verbis eius utamur, "Exibunt angeli et separabunt malos de medio[17] iustorum." Apostoli quoque super sedes xii iudicabunt xii tribus Israel. O quam magna mi-

---

[10] odocet *M3*　[11] *ed.* nihil hominus *M3*　[12] *above* M2　[13] ræstauravit *M3*　[14] suum *M2*　[15] *erasure after* hanc　[16] futuros *M3*　[17] modo *M3*

who saw and heard them but only by common report—yet in his case we have little doubt on the whole that they were true of him, too. Indeed the holy man in his wisdom very clearly teaches that what one sees and admires in others always becomes one's own in turn.[130] And this is none the less true also of the company of angels, whose secrets, as we said before, he investigated,[131] for he states that that which one sees in another refreshes us as much as what one possesses oneself. And to deal with even higher matters, God Almighty, Lord of saints, of angels, and of men, when He had created all things, showed His greatest miracles in those whom He created in His own image. For the angels first announced these things to the best of mankind, and they afterwards announced them to lesser men; this, we read, was so with Moses and the Jewish people and the rest of the saints right until the coming of our Saviour, whose task alone it was and always is to "save that which was lost." So in the beginning He created and in the end he restored the lost. And in this He showed his love to all those to whom He said, "As the Father hath loved Me, even so have I loved you," and He gave them power to perform still greater miracles when He said, "Greater works than these shall ye do." It can be seen that this is entirely true in the matter of teaching too, because Christ undoubtedly won a greater crowd of believers in Himself, not only through His Apostles but through other teachers too. And he will show them the same favour at the future Judgment when it will be the just who are to judge the sinners and when, to use His own words, "The angels shall come forth and sever the wicked from among the just." The Apostles also, sitting on twelve thrones, shall judge the twelve tribes of Israel. O how great and wonderful is the love of Jesus

raque Salvatoris nostri Iesu Christi caritas de qua dixit apostolus, "Ostendit autem suam caritatem Deus in nobis," qui tantam in beato nostro apostolico Gregorio suam ostendit caritatem cuius cum humilitatem fuisset secutus, certum est quod ex ceterorum eum preceptorum custodia, tanta inluminavit sapientia que[18] ipse est; de qua Salamon, "Posside," ait, "sapientiam, et in possessione sua, posside intellegentiam," et reliqua. Quam unde possideri potuisset[19], pater eius exposuit, dicens, "A mandatis tuis intellexi," et paulo prius, "Super omnes docentes me intellexi, quia testimonia tua meditatio mea est: super senes intellexi quia mandata tua exquisivi." Ex hoc igitur, in omnibus apparet sanctis, qualiter quis Christi custodit[20] precepta; hoc mirifico ingenio suo sanctus agnoscendo Gregorius, non[21] de se iactando sed de alio sancto locutus, "Quare," inquit, "divinitatis secreta non nosset, qui divinitatis precepta servaret, cum scriptum sit, 'Qui adheret Domino unus spiritus est?'" Per hunc quippe inhabitantem spiritum eius quo caritas eius diffusa est in corde suo, quę finis precepti est de corde puro et conscientia bona et fide non ficta humilitatis / sue qua proprie caritatis quiescit, opus explevit mirificum.

[*Chapter 31*]

Cur etiam pastoralem fugeret curam, cuius causam gravidinis Iohanni episcopo[1] Ravenensi humiliter reprehendenti[2], pro se apologiticon scripsit. Primo qualis esse debeat pastor populi Dei, super quo sic breviter dixit, "Nequa-

---

[18] q: *M3*   [19] potuisse   [20] costodit *M3*   [21] *insert* a se *M3 then expunged M2*
[1] epi *M3*   [2] den *above M2*

Christ our Saviour of which the Apostle says, "God commendeth his love towards us." Such was the love he showed to our apostolic Gregory when that saint imitated His great humility; and it is certainly true that He who is Himself wisdom illuminated him with such wisdom because he kept the other precepts too. Of this wisdom Solomon says, "With all thy getting, get understanding," and so on. And Solomon's father told him where he could obtain it when he said, "Through Thy precepts I get understanding," and a little before that he says, "I have more understanding than all my teachers; for Thy testimonies are my meditation. I understand more than the ancients because I keep Thy precepts."[132] Thereby it becomes clear in all the saints how far each one is keeping Christ's precepts; so St. Gregory, recognizing this by his own remarkable powers of understanding, though he does not boast about himself, says of another saint, "Why should he not have known the divine secrets when he kept the divine precepts, since it is written that 'he that is joined unto the Lord is one spirit?'" Through this indwelling spirit by which the love of God was shed abroad in his heart, a love which is "the end of the commandment, out of a pure heart and of a good conscience and of faith unfeigned," he completed the marvelous fabric of his own humility on which the fabric of his love rightly rests.[133]

[Chapter 31]

He wrote an apology for himself, explaining why he fled from his pastoral duties, and the reason for his reluctance, when he answered the humble rebuke of Bishop John of Ravenna.[134] First of all, this is what he said about what kind of man a shepherd of the people ought to be; he declared briefly that a man cannot learn humility when he

quam valet in culmine humilitatem discere qui in imis positus non desiit superbire. Inter hec itaque quid sequendum est³ quid tenendum nisi ut virtutibus pollens coactus ad regimen veniat, virtutibus vacuus nec coactus⁴ accedat," deinde miro omnibus modo, qualiter doceat similiter promulgavit. De quo ita quoque breviter dicebat, "Non omnibus una eademque exortatio congruit. Pro qualitate igitur audientium formari debet sermo doctorum. Sepe namque aliis officiunt ⁵ quę aliis prosunt." Hinc etiam diversa humani generis vitia virtutesque⁶ publicando, pene omnium⁷ hominum enumerando genera, quid, cui, quando, quamdiu vel quomodo esset dicendum, mira exortatione admonuit.

[*Chapter 32*]

De fine vero huius vitae viri, quomodo, qualis esset, minime audivimus, quomodo in Deum moritur, ubi maxime queritur sanctitas. Quid amplius fidem nostram primo refecit, quomodo quod ille iam de sua¹ scripsit humilitate monastice vitae, quia mortem quoque que pene cunctis pena est videlicet quasi² ingressum vite et laboris sui premium³ amabat. Hoc enim proprie iam sanctorum est perfectorumque tantum hominum⁴ ita mortem amare et cum apostolo posse dicere, "Cupio dissolvi et esse cum Christo." Mors enim omnium⁵ regina est formidinum, de qua propheta corde divino edoctus dicebat, "Et formido mortis cecidit super me." Secundo, quod hic idem de omnibus sanctis ait propheta communiter, "Pretiosa est in conspec/tu Domini mors sanctorum eius." Iste enim sanctus utique per

---

³ *ed.* et *M3*   ⁴ actus *inserted and erased M3*   ⁵ proficiunt *M3*   ⁶ virtutisque *M3*   ⁷ nium *above M2*   ¹ iam *inserted and erased M3*   ² *ed.* quam si *M2* qualis *M3*   ³ preemium *M3*   ⁴ homine *M3*   ⁵ omn *M3*

reaches the highest office if when he held a very lowly office he never ceased to show pride. Among other matters he explained what would follow and what would be his portion if he did not come to office full of virtue and under compulsion, but if he approached it without virtue and of his own free will; and finally he explained admirably how instruction should be given to all and sundry. On this subject he remarked briefly, "The same exhortation is not suitable for all alike. Therefore a teacher's discourse ought to be constructed according to the nature of his audience. For often things which are profitable to some will be hurtful to others." So, by describing the various vices and virtues of the human race and by enumerating almost all classes of mankind, he showed in a wonderful piece of exposition what should be said, to whom, at what length, and in what manner.[135]

[Chapter 32]

We have heard but little of the form and fashion of Gregory's end or how he died in the Lord—a time when, most of all, holiness is demanded. How much he strengthened our faith in the first place when, while still a humble monk, he wrote and said that he loved death, which in the eyes of almost everyone is a punishment, because he held it to be the entrance to life and the reward of one's labours.[136] Now it is properly the sign only of a saint or of a perfect man to love death thus and to be able to say with the Apostle, "I desire to depart and to be with Christ." For death is the queen of all terrors concerning which the divinely inspired prophet said, "The terrors of death are fallen upon me." Again the prophet says this about all the saints, "Precious in the sight of the Lord is the death of His saints."[137] Now this saint was indeed considered so holy

omnem terram tam sanctus habetur ut semper ab omnibus ubique sanctus Gregorius nominatur. Unde letaniis, quibus Dominum pro nostris imploramus excessibus atque innumeris peccatis quibus eum offendimus, sanctum Gregorium nobis in amminiculum vocamus, cum sanctis scilicet apostolis et martyribus, inter quos[6] eum in celis Christo credimus coniunctum[7] illumque esse super familiam suam servum fidelem et prudentem, qui in tempore tritici[8] tam abundanter donavit illi mensuram, ut cunctis per orbem sacramenta ruminando[9] divina, qualiter illud granum frumenti mortuum multum cadens in terram adferens fructum, a fidelibus cottidie debeat libari atque in perpetuam[10] gustari salutem; quo iam de eo, qui in eo manet et ipse in illo dicebat, "Beatus ille servus quem cum venerit dominus suus invenerit sic facientem. Amen dico vobis, super omnia bona sua constituet eum." Quam scilicet promissionem suam Domini sua beatissimi[11] pretiosa in conspectu eius morte IIII Idus Martias[12] expectat feliciter in ecclesia sancti Petri, cuius sedit episcopatum annos xiii, menses vi dies x, ante eius officii secretarium sepultus, corpore dormit in pace; a quo est resuscitandus in gloriam, cuius corporis et sanguinis secreta nobis initiavit sacramenta, qui solus, remotis omnibus hostiis carnalibus, tollit immolatus omnium peccata; cum quibus omnibus[13] in unitate deitatis suę semper est[14] regnaturus in secula seculorum. Amen.

---

[6] *insert* enim *M3*   [7] convictum *M3*   [8] triticum *M2*   [9] numerando *M3*
[10] perpetuum *M3*   [11] beatissima *M3*   [12] ID. MAR *M3*   [13] *ins. M2*   [14] *del. M2*

throughout the whole world that he is always known to everyone, everywhere, as St. Gregory.[138] Hence in the litanies in which we pray to the Lord, confessing our own excesses and the innumerable sins by which we have offended Him, we call on the support of St. Gregory as well as that of saints, Apostles, and martyrs.[139] We believe indeed that with these he is united to Christ in heaven and that he is that faithful and wise steward, set over His household, who in due season gave all people throughout the world such abundant measure of wheat by his meditations on the divine mysteries that, like the fruit-bearing grain which falls into the ground and dies and yet brings forth much fruit, it is to be daily tasted and enjoyed by the faithful to their eternal salvation. Now about such a man "who dwelleth in Him and He in him," it is said, "Blessed is that servant whom his Lord when He cometh shall find so doing. Verily I say unto you that He shall make him ruler over all His goods." By his death on 12 March, "most precious in His sight,"[140] he awaits in felicity the fulfilment of the promise of his blessed Lord in the Church of St. Peter, where he had his episcopal seat for fourteen years, six months, and ten days.[141] He is buried before the papal vestry,[142] and he sleeps in peace in the body from which he will rise again to the glory of Him who initiated for us the sacramental mysteries of His Body and Blood; Who, setting aside all earthly sacrifices, was alone offered up to bear the sins of all; and with them all He shall reign in the unity of the Godhead, for ever and ever.

AMEN.

Notes

¹ If the author had been writing a prologue according to the regular pattern of saints' Lives written on the Antonian model (see Introduction, p. 48), he would at this point have expressed his unworthiness and incapacity to write the Life of the saint, excusing himself on the ground that he is writing only at the express command of a superior. Though our author several times complains of lack of material, he nowhere, except possibly in c. 30, apologizes for lack of ability in the recognized way. See also c. 3 and p. 141n*11*. Perhaps like Sulpicius himself he did not take such rhetorical commonplaces seriously. Cf. N. K. Chadwick, *Poetry and Letters in Early Christian Gaul* (Cambridge, 1955), p. 110, n. 1. See also *Two Lives*, pp. 60, 310. The title *de vita et virtutibus* is usually part of the title of a saint's Life, though these words may of course have been added later.

² Psa. 77 (78): 7. Biblical references are to the Vulgate. Chapter numbers in parentheses refer to the King James Version. (In some instances the verse number may also differ slightly.)

³ The cult of saints became an outstanding feature of the Church from the third century onwards. At first it was the martyrs the anniversaries of whose death were recorded and whose tombs were visited. When the persecutions ceased, the tombs of other holy men and women also became the centres of cults, honouring those who had practised such austerities and lived such lives of dedication and sacrifice that they achieved the same sanctity as the martyrs themselves. It was from such tombs that relics were obtained; cf. c. 21. As more and more miracles were recorded at certain tombs and as stories spread about the efficacy of the relics, pilgrimages to the saint's body or to the relic became popular and a source of profit to the church which owned them. Hence it became more and more desirable to possess the relic or relics of some saint or martyr. See Introduction, p. 43. The official canonization of saints by the Pope dates only from about the twelfth century. Before that, sainthood was usually established by local tradition and acclamation and was

usually associated with the elevation of the relics. Cf. *Two Lives*, p. 339. The cult of a local saint was liable to spread much further than the locality in which he lived, as in the case of St. Cuthbert and St. Oswald. Needless to say, the existence of a popular Life had a good deal to do with the wider spread of the cult.

⁴ *Lib. Pont.*, ed. Mommsen, p. 161. Neither Bede nor the compiler of the *Liber Pontificalis* knew the name of Gregory's mother. So it was obviously part of the Whitby or Canterbury tradition (see Introduction, p. 53). John the Deacon, writing about 875, was quite familiar with it. He describes in detail the portrait of her which hung in the family mansion on the Caelian Hill (*PL*, LXXV, 229).

⁵ Bede uses a similar phrase about Gregory's ancestry, which made Ewald (p. 44) conclude that Bede had borrowed it from our author. But it is in fact a commonplace of hagiological literature and Bede uses it elsewhere (Brechter, p. 267).

⁶ *Dial.*, I, Pref.: Moricca, p. 14.

⁷ See Introduction, p. 22.

⁸ This long quotation from the introductory letter to the *Moralia* (see Introduction, pp. 22, 29) is also used by Bede in his account of Gregory's life (*HE*, II, 1).

⁹ This simile of the "monastic haven" would appeal especially to a Whitby monk, for the monastery was situated on a high promontory looking far out to sea.

¹⁰ In this quotation (*Epist. ad Leandrum, Moralia: PL*, LXXV, 511) Gregory expresses, as so often elsewhere, his preference for the contemplative rather than the active life. The two forms of Christian life, which were much discussed in the Middle Ages, seem to have been first definitely formulated by Gregory himself. See his *Homilies on Ezekiel*, II, 2: *PL*, LXVI, 952-54. Bede, like Gregory, believed in the superiority of the contemplative life, even though he insisted on the importance of manual labour as part of the monastic rule. This preference was accepted all through the Middle Ages. (Cf. Plummer, II, 68 ff.)

¹¹ The writer seems here to be echoing a phrase from the letter mentioned above with which Sulpicius Severus prefaces his Life of St. Martin, containing the statement, "legentibus consulendum fuit, ne quod his pararet copia congesta fastidium." (Cf. *Two Lives*, p.

62.) But there is no evidence at all that our writer was familiar with this work and, further, Sulpicius is complaining of the wealth of his material, while our writer is making excuses for the lack of it.

[12] This quotation from Psa. 67(68):36 is found very frequently in saints' Lives. "*Sanctis suis*" actually refers to "holy places," but it was invariably taken as referring to the saints.

[13] It was Bede's custom to refer to Rome as the "*sedes apostolica*" and to the Pope as "*papa apostolicus.*" Our writer seems here almost to apologize for giving the title to Gregory.

[14] Our author is echoing Gregory's attitude to miracles, which Gregory puts forward in *Dial.*, I, 12 (Moricca, p. 69), and in several places but especially in his *Homilies on the Gospels*, II, 29: *PL*, LXXVI, 1215 ff., quoted in c. 6. See also c. 6 and notes 18 and 28. Bede, clearly influenced by Gregory, holds similar views. See Plummer, I, lxv, n. 2. Bede also quotes part of Gregory's letter in *HE*, I, 31 (*MGH Epp.*, II, 305-08), in which Gregory counsels Augustine to be humble even though he has been permitted to work miracles.

[15] The use of the word *veritas* as a title of Christ is very frequent in the works of Gregory. He uses it seventeen times in the *Dialogues* and many times elsewhere. Its use is based on the words of Jesus in John 14:6: "Ego sum via, et veritas, et vita."

[16] John 14:12.

[17] Matth. 11:11.

[18] I Cor. 1:22; Matth. 16:4; I Cor. 14:22; the last of the texts here quoted is a favourite one with Gregory, who uses it several times when maintaining his thesis that miracles are intended to win the heathen but that when the church is established they are no longer required. Cf. *Moralia*, XXVII, 12 (*PL, LXXVI*, 420); *Homilies on the Gospels*, 1, 4; 1, 10; II, 29; *PL,* LXXVI, 1091, 1110, 1215.

[19] It was the custom to call the death day of a saint or martyr his *natalicia,* or birthday. Thus Bede in describing his martyrology (*HE*, V, 24) calls it "*martyrologium de nataliciis sanctorum martyrum.*" And in *Opp.* V, 5, he remarks that the day of death is truly the day of birth, "Unde . . . martyrum . . . solennia non funebria sed natalicia dicuntur." Cf. Plummer, I, lxviii, n. 1.

[20] Rom. 8:17.

Notes on pages 81, 83, 85, 87

[21] Luke 8:15; Eph. 5:2.

[22] If the writer is quoting a definite passage from Gregory's writings, I have not been able to identify it. In a letter from Gregory quoted by Bede but not preserved in the papal register (*HE*, I, 23) the Pope, seeking to encourage the failing spirits of Augustine's companions on this mission to England, says, "Though I cannot labour with you, yet because I would have been glad indeed to do so, I hope to share in the joy of your reward." Possibly there was another letter, also not in the papal register (which in any case our author apparently did not know) but preserved at Canterbury, which contained the statement referred to here.

[23] I Cor. 5:3; Matth. 12:29; Eph. 5:8; I Cor. 12:11.

[24] Perhaps a reference to *Homilies on the Gospels*, II, 29: *PL*, LXXVI, 1216), from which the author quotes lower down in the chapter; the sentence runs: "Tanto maiora [miracula] sunt, quanto per haec non corpora sed animae suscitantur." Gregory expresses a very similar idea in *Dialogues*, III, 17 (Moricca, p. 182).

[25] Col. 1:15; Eph. 2:10; James 1:17; Eph. 4:7; I Cor. 12:8-9.

[26] Cf. part of Responsory X for the Sundays in August as found in the Roman breviary, "Homo videt in facie, Deus autem in corde" —a passage closer to our writer's words than the passage he may have had in mind, I Sam. 16:7.

[27] Col. 2:3.

[28] The writer is quoting from the *Homilies on the Gospels*, II, 29: *PL*, LXXVI, 1216. This is a homily on Mark 16:14-20, in which Gregory uses verse 17 as the basis for one of his longer disquisitions on the subject of the value of miracles.

[29] Psa. 6:9; see also Matth. 14:29 and Acts 13:11.

[30] Matth. 11:29; Acts 9:41; Luke 21:19.

[31] *Dial*. I, 2: Moricca, p. 23.

[32] Matth. 18:1.

[33] Gregory's reluctance to be made Pope is in accordance with the attitude of a large number of saints when faced with the prospect of being made bishops. Thus Martin and Athanasius, Ambrose and Augustine of Hippo all had to be compelled to accept the office. The same is true of Anglo-Saxon saints such as Cuthbert and Chad, Wilfrid and Dunstan. One of the most extraordinary of these

constantly recurring stories concerns Ammonius, a monk of Nitria, who cut off one of his ears and even threatened to cut out his tongue to avoid being consecrated bishop. Cf. *DCB*, I, 102, and *Two Lives*, p. 330. So he was left to his life of contemplation. Generally, as in the case of Gregory, the reluctance was due partly to a sense of unworthiness and partly to the desire for the contemplative rather than the active life. This story of his attempts to avoid the papacy is borrowed both by Paul the Deacon's Interpolator and by John the Deacon. See *PL*, LXXV, 48, 81.

[34] Luke 2:37.

[35] Gen. 28:12, 17, 19; Psa. 17 (18):12; Matth. 5:15.

[36] I have not been able to identify the quotation from St. Jerome.

[37] Heb. 9:11, 12; Phil. 2:8; John 6:15; John 12:36; Matth. 26:39.

[38] Phil. 2:7-8 and *Homilies on the Gospels*, II, 27: *PL*, LXXVI, 1209.

[39] I John 4:17; cf. I Cor. 13:1-3; Malachi 2:6; Psa. 18 (19):9.

[40] The gift of prophecy was a sign of increasing spiritual power, as Gregory points out in his account of St. Benedict (*Dialogues* II, 11: Moricca, p. 98).

[41] If the incident is based on actuality, it must have happened some years before Gregory became Pope. Bede tells the story but with certain differences (*HE*, II, 1). Both he and our author declare it to be traditional. Bede describes the boys as having "fair complexions, handsome faces, and lovely hair." Our writer is uncertain whether they were "beautiful boys" or "curly-haired, handsome youths." According to Bede, Gregory went to the marketplace to see them, whereas our author suggests that they were brought to him. Another curious feature of this account is that Gregory spoke directly to the youths and received direct answers, undeterred by language difficulties. Bede, less naïvely, makes it clear that the information about their race and so forth came from those who stood by. Paul the Deacon follows Bede entirely in his account of the incident.

[42] The scribe uses the form *Anguli* throughout except in c. 6, where he writes *Angli* but crosses the *l*. In two instances the corrector (see Introduction, pp. 68-69) has expunged the *u* (cc. 12, 13). Bede uses only the form *Angl-*, though he refers to the land from which the Angli come as *Angulus* (*HE*, I, 15). But whether or not

the Whitby author himself used the form *Anguli* it is clear from a statement in c. 13 that he treated the form as a dissyllable when he remarks that *Angulorum* with the *addition* of a single letter becomes *angelorum*. It is clear, too, that though the Angli whom Gregory saw in Rome were Northumbrians, the writer uses the term in a general sense just as Bede does, for in c. 12 he refers to Æthelberht, King of Kent, as *rex Angulorum*. See W. Levison, *England and the Continent*, p. 92 and n.1. Gregory himself addressed Æthelberht as *"regi Anglorum"* (*HE*, I, 32).

⁴³ In the *Moralia*, XXVII, 11: *PL*, LXXVI, 411, Gregory declares that East and West are joined in one faith and that the language of Britain, which once could make only barbarous noises, had now begun to sing the Hebrew *Alleluia* in its divine praises. One is tempted to think that this remark may be the starting point of the famous story. Add to this Gregory's letter in 595 (*MGH Epp.* I, 388 f.) in which he ordered the priest Candidus, who was setting out for Gaul, to buy in the slave-markets English boys, aged about seventeen to eighteen years, so that they might be trained in Roman monasteries, presumably to be sent back as missionaries to England. Though this particular letter may not have been known, yet the custom of buying or ransoming slaves to turn into missionaries was known. Aidan ransomed slave boys for this purpose (*HE*, III, 5), while Willibrord seized thirty Danish boys, baptized them, and took them to the Frankish kingdom, presumably to be trained for the same purpose. (Alcuin, *Life of Willibrord*, c. 9: *EHD I*, 714.) So some ingenious Northumbrian monk may well have invented the story as part of the Gregory saga. The fact that Bede knows it in a slightly different form suggests that it was well established when our author wrote it down.

⁴⁴ See Introduction, p. 1. The name *Dere* was a collective name given to the Anglian tribe that settled in the center and east of what is now called Yorkshire. It is derived from the British word *deifr*, meaning "water." Cf. Stenton, p. 74.

⁴⁵ Benedict I was Pope from 575 to 579. Presumably by this time Gregory had become a monk in the monastery of St. Andrew. See Introduction, p. 21.

⁴⁶ The use of the word *vasis* suggests that Gregory was echoing

St. Paul's expression in Rom. 9:22, *"vasa irae apta in interitum,"* "vessels of wrath, fitted for destruction."

[47] The story of the people's appeal to the Pope, with the threefold division of the crowds and the threefold cry, bears all the marks of legend. It is borrowed by the Interpolator of Paul the Deacon's Life (c. 19: *PL,* LXXV, 51), who varies the third cry to "Gregorium non tam dimisisti quam expulisti," thereby spoiling the correspondence of the three cries. John the Deacon also spoils the story slightly by joining the second and third cries with *quia.* If Bede had known this picturesque little story, he would surely have inserted it into his *History.*

[48] The original form of the phrase was probably *loco sta, loco* being a locative. The form in which our author quotes it is one which would be more familiar to him, for he was no Latinist. The story was apparently unknown to Bede; otherwise he would probably have used it. It may well owe its origin to the hypothetical monk with a taste for puns who perhaps was responsible for the more famous series of puns in c. 9. Cf. p. 145n43.

[49] Benedict died in 579. The author omits altogether the pontificate of Pelagius II (579-90). It was during his reign that Gregory spent nearly seven years in Constantinople. See Introduction, p. 22. From 585 to the time of his ascent to the papal throne in 590 Gregory was in his monastery. Even then, it was six years before Augustine set out for Britain, so that apparently our author hardly realized how long the delay was when he speaks of *"quantaque potuit festinatione."*

[50] If the writer had been familiar with Gregory's correspondence, he would have been able to correct his facts as Bede was able to do. To begin with, the Whitby monk does not realize what is made clear by Gregory's correspondence, that there were two missionary expeditions, one in 597, when (as we learn from Bede) Augustine came accompanied by Laurentius, and the second in 601, when Mellitus came, also accompanied by Laurentius, who had in the meantime returned from Britain with a priest called Peter to report progress. Paulinus also accompanied the second expedition, as we learn from *HE,* I, 29. The *Liber Pontificalis* (ed. Mommsen, p. 161) also reports only one expedition and gives the names of the

missionaries as *"Mellitus, Augustine et Johannes."* It may be that this was the source of our author's confusion, though the rest of his story also differs from what was doubtless the true history of events as recorded by Bede. The latter agrees with the Whitby monk in saying that Augustine consecrated Mellitus (*HE*, II, 3), who was appointed Bishop of the East Saxons. But, on the other hand, Bede clearly states that Laurentius was consecrated by Augustine with a view to his being the Archbishop's successor, and, when the latter died in 604, Laurentius duly succeeded him (*HE*, II, 4). See Introduction, pp. 53, 57.

[51] See Introduction, p. 1. If the story of the young Deirans had been more than a legend one would have expected that some effort would have been made to evangelize Northumbria soon after Augustine's arrival. But according to Bede the initiative came from Edwin himself, and it was not until 625 that he finally accepted Christianity, nearly thirty years after Augustine's arrival. But there were good reasons why Gregory should have sent his missionaries first to the court of King Æthelberht at Canterbury. For one thing Kent was the first kingdom that any traveler from the Continent would normally come to. Secondly, Æthelberht was one of the seven great English kings in Bede's famous list (*HE*, II, 5) who held the *imperium* or overlordship over the Saxon kingdoms and whom the *ASC* calls the *Bretwaldan*. And in addition Æthelberht had connections with the Continent, for his wife Bertha was the daughter of Charibert, King of Paris, who ruled over western Gaul down to the Pyrenees. She was a Christian and so could be expected to give help in the conversion of her husband and his people and so be of much assistance to Augustine in the early days of the mission. Æthelberht was no ignorant pagan but a man of enlightenment who was responsible for the earliest code of laws we possess (*EHD I*, 357-59).

[52] See the previous note. Edwin is the fifth in Bede's list of *Bretwaldan*. Except for the Northumbrian kings, Edwin and Oswald and, for a short time, Oswiu, the *imperium* did not extend north of the Humber, a river which for more than two centuries maintained a clear distinction between the northern and southern peoples. The term *Humbrenses* is here used to denote all the English

people to the north of the river. The regular name, used as early as 672 for the latter, was *Nordanhymbrorum gens*, the form used by Bede (see Stenton, pp. 32 ff.). Eddius uses the less precise form *Ultrahumbrenses*. The form *Humbrenses* is rarely used elsewhere. Indeed our author's use of this vague term may well be adduced as an additional reason to show his ignorance of Bede's *History* (see p. 57). It would seem that the Whitby monk was familiar with the extent of Edwin's sway during his time of greatness. The description of it in Bede (*HE*, II, 16) reads like part of a saga in which Edwin played the role of the Christian warrior king of the Beowulf type.

[53] Rev. 19:6.

[54] Psa. 88 (89):6.

[55] Matth. 11:28.

[56] The Old English forms of the name, *Eadwine*, had three syllables.

[57] Such elaborate explanations of the spiritual meaning of names and words are typical of the theological symbolism popular with both Gregory and Bede. Cf. *BLTW*, 173 ff. As Gasquet points out (p. 17, n. 5), the symbolic interpretation rests solely on the correspondence of the number of syllables in the word *Alleluia* with the number of Persons in the Trinity. See Heb. 7:10; Rom. 9:23; Matth. 28:19.

[58] See note 57. Our author, like Bede, does not mention and possibly had never heard the story which appears in sources of uncertain date (Nennius, *Historia Brittonum*, c. 63, *MGH Auct. Ant.*, XIII, 206), that Edwin and his daughter Eanflæd, together with 10,000 of Edwin's people, were baptized by a certain British priest named Rum map Urbgen (or Rhun, the son of Urien). The story may well have been invented after the time of our author and Bede. No British tradition was likely to admit that Paulinus was responsible for the conversion of Northumbria. The peculiar way in which the story is told ("If anyone wants to know who baptized them, it was Rum map Urbgen who baptized them") seems to imply that the writer is trying to make a point rather than tell sober history. Cf. *Celt and Saxon*, p. 32, and p. 50, n. 2.

[59] The writer is probably referring to such marriages as are

dealt with in the answers to the questions which Augustine sent to Pope Gregory, a book called the *Libellus Responsionum*, which had a wide circulation and was incorporated by Bede into his *History* (*HE*, I, 27). Again, our author seems not to have known this book. The fifth answer is generally supposed not to have been written by Gregory. It is a reply to Augustine's question as to whether a man may marry his stepmother or his sister-in-law. The question of the legality of the marriage of first cousins is also raised. Marriage with a stepmother was common among Germanic peoples. Eanbald, son of Æthelberht, King of Kent, for example, married his stepmother (*HE*, II, 5), and the practice continued until much later (Plummer, II, 48, 88). Wihtred, King of Kent, in his code of laws drawn up in 695, also warns his people against unlawful marriages (*EHD I*, 362).

[60] The Germanic peoples, as Tacitus observed (*Germania*, c. 10), were much given to studying omens, and he also refers to their practice of consulting the cries and the flight of birds. In Roman times the appearance of a crow on the left-hand side was considered a favourable omen. Cf. Virgil, *Eclogues*, IX, 15, and Cicero, *De divinatione*, I, 39, 85. So possibly the crow may have appeared on the right side.

[61] Psa. 39 (40):4.

[62] Gen. 1:28.

[63] The author was evidently familiar with more than one form of the story; but he is careful not to claim too much for the version that he decides to tell. Bede tells the story in a much more dramatic and interesting form than does our author. Cf. *HE*, II, 12.

[64] The incident must have happened shortly before Edwin, with Rædwald's help, overthrew Æthelfrith at the Battle of the River Idle in 617. If, as the writer asserts, none of the people who were living at the time of the incident were still alive and presumably able to remember it, then this passage could have been written any time after 700—always provided that our author's statement is accurate. See Introduction, p. 48.

[65] In the manuscript Rædwald is wrongly described as King of the West Angles. This was undoubtedly due to a mistake on the part of the Continental scribe who made the copy which has sur-

vived, rather than to a mistake of the author. See Introduction, p. 69.

⁶⁶ I Thess. 1:10.

⁶⁷ Bede's account of the incident nowhere states that the mysterious visitor was Paulinus himself.

⁶⁸ It is not uncommon in hagiographical literature for the souls of the saints to be seen departing from the body at the time of death in the form of a dove. St. Benedict, for instance, saw the soul of his sister Scholastica departing in this form; and a dove was also seen issuing from the mouth of the priest named Spes, as he died (*Dialogues*, II, 34; IV, 11: Moricca, pp. 127, 242). The swan played a large part in the folklore of the north and the *fylgja*, or accompanying spirit, which, according to the Norse sagas, left the body at death, was occasionally seen in the form of a swan. In view of Paulinus's close association with Lincoln (*HE*, II, 16), it might be due to the survival of a local tradition of this sort that St. Hugh of Lincoln, the bishop there from 1186 to 1200, is the only English saint whose emblem is a swan, though the popular explanation of this was that the saint was constantly accompanied by a pet swan.

⁶⁹ The "South English" to a writer north of the Humber would mean the inhabitants of any part of England south of that river. Probably, therefore, our writer means that the incident happened in some monastery south of the Humber. Cf. Stenton, p. 33. It is difficult to explain why the corrector of the manuscript changed the original form *Sudranglorum* to *Sundaranglorum*. He may have been bothered by the *r* of *Sudr-*, having already removed the *r* from *Vestranglorum* in c. 16. So in this case he changed *Sudr* to *Sundar*, a form familiar to him. Though the corrector was probably not aware of the fact, the form, which is not found elsewhere, expresses the political situation quite well.

⁷⁰ The importance of this sentence in assessing the date of the *Life* is discussed in the Introduction, pp. 47-48.

⁷¹ Lindsey was in early days associated with the people whom Bede calls the *Lindisfari*, not to be confused with the inhabitants of the island of Lindisfarne, whom he calls *Lindisfarnenses*. The province of Lindsey lay between the Humber and the Witham and

was continually in dispute between the kings of Mercia and Northumbria. See Introduction, p. 42. The monastery of Bardney was in this district, but it is not likely that Trimma came from there, as the story stresses the fact that he was unfamiliar with Lindsey. Hatfield Chase, usually presumed to be the site of Edwin's last battle (*Hedfled* in the text), is a stretch of land near Hatfield, a village in the West Riding of Yorkshire, and is now just outside the present boundary of Lindsey. This story seems to strengthen the usual identification of the site of the battle. The route from Hatfield Chase to Whitby would pass through Goodmanham near Market Weighton, where Edwin ordered the heathen temples to be destroyed in 625 (*HE*, II, 13), and so on through Pickering to Whitby, leading mostly along Roman roads. The distance would be about 70 miles.

[72] Professor Whitelock points out (*EHD I*, 689, n. 7) that "*maritus*" is our author's way of rendering the word *ceorl*, which in Old English means not only married man but also peasant proprietor, the sense in which it is used here. There is an echo of Acts 9:11.

[73] Ecclesiasticus 34:7.

[74] The scourging of saints and others in a vision or a dream is not infrequent in saints' Lives. One of the best-known examples is that of Laurentius, described by Bede (*HE*, II, 6); other instances are Natalius, who, according to Eusebius (*Historia ecclesiastica*, V, 28) was scourged all night by angels. Jerome was taken before the Divine Judge and scourged for his love of heathen literature (*Epp.*, XXII, 30: *PL*, XXII, 416), while Adamnan in his *Life of St. Columba* (III, 6) describes how the saint was struck by an angel with a whip for refusing to obey a command. He carried the scar with him through life.

[75] More churches seem to have been dedicated to St. Peter in England than to any other saint during the seventh and eighth centuries. They include York, Lindisfarne, Peterborough and its daughter churches, as well as Ripon, Selsey, and Wearmouth. Cf. W. Levison, *England and the Continent*, pp. 35, 260 f.

[76] Gregory held strong views about the necessity of baptism as a means of salvation. Even unbaptized babies, he held, were doomed

to eternal torments (*Moralia*, II, 21: *PL*, LXXV, 877). So our author, who doubtless agreed, is making it clear that these revenants were Christians killed at the Battle of Hatfield Chase.

[77] At this point the second part of the *Life* begins and the writer turns back to the story of St. Gregory. The close association of the relics of Edwin with the Gregory altar would make the arrangement of the *Life* seem logical, at any rate to those who read it or heard it read at Whitby. The stories that follow in cc. 20-23 and 28-29 have all been borrowed by the Interpolator who added to the original Life written by Paul the Deacon (cc. 23-29: *PL*, LXXV, 52-58), while cc. 20, 21, 22, and 29 have been incorporated by John the Deacon into his Life (II, 41-44: *PL*, LXXV, 103-06). There is no doubt about the source of each, for the verbal borrowings and even the order of the stories are unmistakable proof. As John tells us, he bases them on the lessons read in the English churches. See Introduction, p. 59. This story, probably through the medium of John's Life and the very popular Life of Paul the Deacon in its interpolated form became well known throughout the Middle Ages and was incorporated in *The Golden Legend*. It was also a favourite subject for painters in England and on the Continent. It is represented in several wall-paintings in English churches as, for example, at Beverstone in Gloucestershire, Slapton in Northamptonshire, Stoke Charity in Hampshire, Paignton in Devon, and Wyverstone in Suffolk. The story is also interesting in that it demonstrates that the doctrine of transubstantiation was held in the seventh century by the English Church.

[78] The words of administration of the communion as given here were presumably the words used in the English Church in the late seventh and early eighth century, though this is the only evidence. John the Deacon copies the words used here, but the Interpolator uses another formula, "Corpus Domini Christi prosit tibi in remissionem omnium peccatorum." Possibly this was the form of words used in Rome, or wherever the Interpolator worked over Paul's Life at the end of the ninth century. It is not safe to conclude as writers have usually done that the formula used here was used in Rome in John's time, seeing that John is borrowing verbally from the Whitby *Life*.

[79] John the Deacon says that Gregory placed the bread *"super altare,"* but Paul says he covered it with a *"corporalis palla."* It was probably some kind of corporal, for the word *vestimentum* is used in ecclesiastical Latin not only of a vestment but also of an altar-cloth.

[80] Matth. 16:17.

[81] John 6:54.

[82] John 6:57.

[83] This story is one of the series for which a definite source can be found. In 594 Constantina, wife of the Emperor Mauricius Tiberius, sent to Gregory asking for St. Paul's head or some part of his body for a new church which she was having built. The Pope answered politely that it was not the Roman custom to venture to touch any part of a saint's body when asked for relics of him but only to send associated objects. He then went on to tell how during the time of Pope Leo I some Greeks asked for relics and were given some clothes, for in the West it would be considered an intolerable sacrilege to interfere with the bodies of saints. When the Greeks cut the clothes, blood ran from them, thus proving their authenticity (*MGH Epp.* I, 264 ff.). John the Deacon repeats the Whitby story but also refers to this other incident. Though it is true that in Western Europe strict Roman laws protected the bodies of the saints in the early centuries, yet by the middle of the fourth century these bodies were frequently translated and though Gregory might protest, the indignation of the envoys here mentioned is proof enough of the importance attached to some part of the body. Relics were considered essential in the consecration of a new church, and the crypts still to be seen in the cathedrals at Ripon and Hexham are the places built by St. Wilfrid for the deposition and exhibition of relics brought by him from Rome in the seventh century. For further information see the article on Relics, *ERE*, X, 653.

[84] Rom. 14:23; Acts 15:9.

[85] Psa. 67 (68):36.

[86] Acts 10:34, 35.

[87] On this and similar phrases see c. 1 and note. Gregory uses a like phrase of Crisaurius in *Dialogues*, IV, 40 (Moricca, p. 293) and repeats it in *Homilies on the Gospels*, I, 12: *PL*, LXXVI, 1122.

[88] Gal. 1:16.

[89] Both the Interpolator and John the Deacon mistake the meaning of the "high place" in their versions of this story, supposing it to mean that the magicians were placed in a position from which they could easily identify Gregory in the procession, but the high place was chosen to strengthen the magic spell. Compare the story told by Eddius (c. 13) of how when Wilfrid was wrecked on the shores of Sussex returning from Gaul in 666, the local magician took up his stand on a high mound. This feature is also found in Norse witchcraft. (Eddius, p. 160.)

[90] Eph. 6:13.

[91] Col. 2:12.

[92] Again the Interpolator and John the Deacon are in difficulties about the meaning of the obscure last sentence; both interpret it to mean that the magicians themselves were made beneficiaries of the church funds, but this would hardly fit in with the phrase which makes them *"pro Domino medicos animarum."* The phrase *"medicus animarum"* occurs in Aldhelm's famous letter to Gerontius (*MGH Auct. Ant.*, XV, 484).

[93] See previous note.

[94] The story refers to an incident in 593 when Agilulf, King of the Lombards, marched upon the gates of Rome. Gregory refers to the incident in his Preface to the second book of his *Homilies on Ezekiel* (*PL*, LXXVI, 934), and in the pathetic sentences with which he excuses himself in the last of the Homilies for bringing them to an end (*PL*, LXXVI, 1072). Agilulf marched away again, according to our author, after listening to the pleadings of Gregory. The same story is told in Prosper's Continuation (*MGH Auct. Ant.*, II, 339) and in the Life of John the Deacon (IV, 13: *PL*, LXXV, 182). Gregory never mentions the incident himself in his letters or elsewhere; the account of Pope Leo I's pleading with Attila and the Huns is so similar that one is tempted to treat this story, as Ewald does (*MGH Epp.*, I, 319 n.) as a mere repetition of the same incident in a different dress.

[95] Psa. 45 (46):5-7.

[96] The author is not making a pun here on "rustic speech" and "rustic diet" as one might easily suppose, knowing our author's

weakness for puns, but he is simply quoting Gregory (*Dial.*, Pref.: Moricca, p. 16) and apologizing for the fact that it is not always possible or even suitable to quote the exact words of the various characters in his stories, because by so doing, he might lose the point of the anecdote by overloading it with details.

[97] The writer is referring to Gregory's forty *Homilies on the Gospels,* which were composed to be read at Mass, the first book being read to the congregation by papal notaries, while the twenty which follow and form the second book were read by Gregory himself. They were edited and published in 593 with an introductory letter to Secundinus, Bishop of Taormina in Sicily.

[98] Mark 16:15; I Cor. 2:7.

[99] The title "golden-mouthed" is usually associated with John Chrysostom (347-407), the famous preacher of Antioch and Patriarch of Constantinople. Exactly how the epithet arose is not known, but from the fifth century the term came to be used by the Greeks of any favourite orator. In a study of "The Prose of Alfred's Reign" (*Continuations and Beginnings,* ed. E. G. Stanley, London, 1966), Professor Whitelock points out that Bishop Wærferth of Worcester in his translation of Gregory's *Dialogues* uses the same expression (p. 77). In this work, which he did at King Alfred's request somewhere about 890, he refers in two places to Gregory as golden-mouthed and in one place could almost be quoting from our *Life* when he says "whom the Romans call 'golden-mouthed' because of the grace of his fair speech." Since neither Paul the Deacon nor John the Deacon seems to have known this title for Gregory, there is a possibility that Wærferth, who was Bishop of Worcester from 873 to 915, was familiar with this *Life*. Oftfor, a pupil of St. Hild's, was Bishop of Worcester from 691 to 963, so that a copy of the *Life* might possibly have found its way to Worcester, if not during his period of rule yet at a later time. As Offa, King of Mercia, possessed a copy of Bede's *Ecclesiastical History,* there seems no reason why a copy of the *Life* should not have been found at Worcester. And in the next century traditions of Gregory known to our author were known in Worcester too (see p. 160n*120*).

[100] Prov. 21:20 and 14:33; Psa. 44 (45):3.

[101] This is the second quotation from Jerome (Epistle 46: *PL,*

XXII, 485), the other being in c. 7. It would suggest that some of Jerome's works were available at Whitby. Bede was very familiar with his writings as well as those of Gregory, Ambrose, and Augustine.

[102] Matth. 5:14, 16; Luke 12:8.

[103] One of Gregory's *Homilies on the Gospels* (II, 34: *PL*, XXVI, 1246-59) acquired special fame because he enumerated the nine orders of angels in it. This division of the angelic hosts was accepted all through the Middle Ages; Dante refers to it, and it even found its way into *Paradise Lost* (V, line 600). The division of the angels into three hierarchies of three orders each first appeared in the treatise on the hierarchies of heaven written by Dionysius the Areopagite (*PG*, III, 199 ff.). The first hierarchy consisted of cherubim, seraphim, and thrones; the second of dominions, virtues, powers; the third, of principalities, archangels, and angels. There were originally ten orders, but, as Gregory points out, like the ten pieces of silver in the parable (Luke 15:8, 9) one was lost when Satan and his followers fell from heaven. Ælfflæd of Whitby was of course familiar with this division and adjured St. Cuthbert by the nine orders of angels to tell her about the fate of her brother Ecgfrith. See Introduction, p. 41, and *Two Lives*, pp. 102, 328.

[104] John 7:38.

[105] It is possible, as Gasquet points out (p. 33, n. 6), that this is a reference to a remark of Augustine in his *De civitate Dei* (Book XV: *PL*, XLI, 437), "*sive in angelis quorum numerus ignoratur a nobis.*" But there are other statements, too, to the same effect, e.g., *De Trinitate*, Book III, 10, 21: *PL*, XLII, 881.

[106] Matth. 5:8; 13:52; 6:20.

[107] Ezekiel 1:25; *Homilies on Ezekiel*, I, 8: *PL*, LXXVI, 859. Gregory edited two books of *Homilies on Ezekiel*, the first consisting of twelve sermons, the second of ten. Our author concerns himself chiefly with the eighth homily of the first book (*PL*, LXXVI, 859). See Introduction, p. 30, and p. 154n94, and E. S. Duckett, *The Gateway to the Middle Ages*, pp. 559 ff.

[108] By "*celum*" the writer means the firmament or sky, while "*celos*" means the heavenly regions which were opened up to allow the descent of the dove.

[109] Matth. 3:16.

[110] The story of the white dove's dictating the *Homilies on Ezekiel* is told by the Interpolator (c. 28: *PL*, LXXV, 57-58), but John the Deacon tells the story in a different form (*PL*, LXXV, 221-22). He relates that after Gregory's death a famine took place that was attributed by the Roman people to Gregory's extravagance during his lifetime. Wishing to show their resentment, they decided to burn his books, for he had left no other possessions. But Peter, his friend of the *Dialogues,* intervened, telling the people the story of how he had seen the Holy Spirit in the form of a dove, hovering above his head as he wrote. As Peter begged the people very earnestly to refrain from this sacrilegious act, he fell dead in the pulpit. His death was taken as a sign of the truth of his testimony and the books were spared. John adds that this is the reason why Gregory is always represented with a dove hovering round his head. But when giving a detailed description of the portrait which hung in the monastery of St. Andrew, John does not mention the dove (*PL*, LXXV, 230-31). But there is preserved in a book published in the seventeenth century (*Hierolexicon* [Rome, 1677], *s. v. baculum*, p. 65), a copy of a drawing in which the dove is seen, made by a certain Ciacconius (Alfonso Chacon), a sixteenth-century Spanish savant and antiquarian, that may possibly be linked with this original painting. See Paul Meyvaert, *Bede and Gregory the Great*, Jarrow Lecture, 1964, Plate II and note 17, pp. 21-22.

[111] The familiar friend was obviously Peter the Deacon. This attitude to those who intrude upon a saint's privacy and see him associated with some supernatural phenomenon is very common in saints' Lives. It is also a commonplace for saints to forbid those who have witnessed a miracle to mention it until after the saint's death. The tradition may derive from the command of Jesus to his disciples on the Mount of Transfiguration (Matth. 17: 9). Bede quotes the passage when describing a miracle connected with St. Cuthbert. See *Two Lives,* pp. 191, 319-20.

[112] As Jones suggests (*Saints' Lives and Chronicles,* p. 114, n. 76), the basis of this mysterious sentence is probably the verses in II Cor. 6: 7-8, "on the right hand and the left, by honour and dishonour." If so, our author is clearly misinterpreting the passage

to suit his context, which he was quite capable of doing. The right hand, as in the parable of the sheep and goats (Matth. 25:33) and very frequently elsewhere in the Scriptures and especially in the Psalms, is the place of honour. It was on the right hand of the altar that the saints such as Cuthbert, Aidan, and Cedd were buried. But the left side is the side of the lost souls, as in the above-mentioned parable. It was in Roman times generally the side of ill-omen, as the derivation of the word *sinister* proves. See *sinister* in the O.E.D.

[113] The reading *"plenitudo"* is vouched for by the fact that in a number of places Gregory explains the significance of the cherubim as the *"plenitudo scientiae."* Besides the passage quoted, *Homilies on Ezekiel*, II, 9: *PL,* LXXVI, 1054, see also *PL,* LXXVI, 666, 1141, 1191, 1253.

[114] See c. 7, also probably another reference to the angels mentioned in c. 25.

[115] Job 38:3.

[116] This quotation from the epistle to Leander which prefaces his *Moralia* (*PL,* LXXV, 515) is one of the numerous places in which Gregory complains of constant ill-health. One of the most vivid references is in his letter to Marianus, Bishop of Arabia (*MGH Epp.*, II, 281). In it he mentions his gout and a strange and painful fire that sometimes spreads through the whole body. "To put it briefly, I am so full of the infection of a noxious humour that it is a punishment for me to live and I eagerly long for death, the only remedy for my troubles." See Introduction, p. 30.

[117] The practice of medicine in monasteries was widespread throughout the Middle Ages. In the *Anonymous Life of St. Cuthbert* (IV, 17; *Two Lives*, p. 137) we read of the skilled physicians in the monastery of Lindisfarne. Sick people came to Iona for medical attention (Adamnan, *Life of St. Columba*, I, 21). See also *HE,* IV, 19; V, 2, 6.

[118] The writer is retelling the story of Justus which Gregory relates in the *Dialogues* (IV, 57: Moricca, p. 317). But he spoils the whole spirit of it. In Gregory's own account he is not, as here, showing off his powers of binding and loosing souls in hell, but acting as a kindly superior, imposing expiation according to the

methods and standards of his day. In the original story the three coins are *aureos solidos*.

[119] Matth. 16:18; Psa. 87 (88):6.

[120] The whole of this passage about Jerome is obscure, partly because of the extremely involved style in which it is written, though one must not rule out the possibility of the text being corrupt. But it is also due to the fact that the author is referring to a story about Jerome which seems to have been known in the north of England and perhaps Mercia but not elsewhere. By good fortune this story has been preserved in the margin of a twelfth-century MS now in the Cambridge University Library (Kk. 4.6). The manuscript, which comes from Worcester, is of mixed contents, mostly theological, and contains a copy of the *Liber Pontificalis* in its second form, the form known both to Bede and to our author. It reaches as far as the year 715. On the margin of f. 233, near the section dealing with the life of Pope Siricius, is an insertion in which the writer begins by saying that he has extracted it from the "*dicta regis Alfredi veridicis*" and then goes on to tell the story of how Jerome came to Siricius bearing a copy of his translation of the Bible. On being told that a learned monk wished to see him, Siricius told his attendants to bring him in. But when those present saw Jerome clad in rough skins they all despised him and so he left the presence. On the following day he dressed himself in very costly garments, so that everyone gazed on him with admiration as he crossed the Forum. A certain cardinal met him and invited Jerome to come with him to the papal palace. This time Jerome was welcomed with the greatest honour and placed on a seat beside Siricius. As various dainties were brought to Jerome, he gazed reverently at the costly garments he was wearing and finally bent his head and kissed his own robes. When those around asked Jerome what he was doing, the saint answered that he himself honoured those things which brought him honour—namely, his rich clothes. Hereupon the Pope and the whole papal court were enraged and the light of the world was driven from the capital city of the world "*a mundi capite lux mundi pellitur urbe.*"

The continuation of the story appears on f. 244 v. in the margin

Note on page 127

close by the Life of St. Gregory and in the same twelfth-century hand. It relates how it was an ancient custom in Rome for lights to burn day and night over the tombs of the Popes; and not undeservedly (*nec immerito,* a favourite phrase of our author and St. Gregory), for, according to the Gospel, it is to these that the keys are entrusted with which to bind and unbind. The custom fell into disuse—whether from poverty or negligence, the writer is unable to say. But that burning and shining light Gregory, while he was Pope, either read or heard of the way Siricius had treated Jerome. One day when he was wandering around the tombs of the Popes, he came across that of Siricius. "This tomb," he exclaimed, "holds that Pope who once drove forth from the city the light of the world that fills the world with God's word. It is wrong that a light should shine on his tomb." With these words he broke the vessel with his staff and spilled the oil. Thus he avenged Jerome on Siricius.

The story is written in a kind of loose metrical prose with occasional rhyme. It can hardly have been derived from the Whitby *Life,* for it would not be possible to derive an ordered narrative from the confused allusions in the text. It is more likely, as Professor Whitelock suggests, that it may have been derived from some lost Life of Jerome, known at Whitby; or it could be part of the Gregory saga on which the author based his Life that found its way to Worcester (see p. 155n99) and came to be incorporated in the "dicta" of Alfred, of which a copy seems to have been preserved in Worcester. Cf. Miss Whitelock's article on "The Prose of Alfred's Reign," *Continuations and Beginnings* (London, 1966) pp. 72-73.

Though the story is certainly legendary, it has some slight historical basis, for Jerome, while living in Rome, had aroused such feeling against himself that he was compelled to leave the city when Siricius, who had little sympathy with him, succeeded Jerome's friend Damasus as Pope. The story clearly fits in with the context, placed as it is between the anecdote which illustrates the Pope's powers of binding and loosing (referred to in the "dicta" anecdote) and another story which relates how Gregory dealt with predecessors of whom he did not approve. None of the other Lives of Gregory refer to the incident and so far as I know it is not related

Notes on page 127

elsewhere. For a full account of the Cambridge MS and a transcript of the Jerome story see W. Levison, "Aus englischen Bibliotheken II," *Neues Archiv der Gesellschaft für altere deutsche Geschichtskunde*, XXXV (1910), 424-27.

[121] This story appears in the Interpolation in Paul's Life, but it is told somewhat differently in John's Life, following what was doubtless the Roman tradition of the famine after Gregory's death; the sequel of the story has already been described, p. 157n*110*. Gregory's successor was Sabinianus, of whom little is known except that he was elected five months after Gregory's death and ruled for just under eighteen months. The manner of his death is variously described, but the general impression given by historians is that he was mean and penurious in dealing with the citizens. The *Liber Pontificalis* (ed. Mommsen, p. 163) describes how he sold wheat from the pontifical storehouses. In the same place it is said that his funeral procession was taken *(eiectus)* through St. John's Gate and outside the city walls by the *pons Mulvia*, presumably to avoid demonstrations on the part of angry citizens; he was buried in St. Peter's Church. Our author's story was known to later historians presumably from the interpolated version of Paul's Life, but it is a crude and unworthy tale in which Gregory's only motive is revenge. Nowhere in the *Life* does the Whitby author reveal more clearly the crudeness of his times. In fact the dead saint's violent behaviour is reminiscent of northern tales told later on in the Norse sagas of the frightful havoc wrought by offended ghosts upon the living as in the *Grettissaga* or the *Eyrbyggja Saga*. Cf. Hastings, *ERE*, XII, 126.

[122] This story about Trajan was widely spread and gave rise to much discussion through the Middle Ages, mostly because it was retold by John the Deacon; so both the story and the doubts he expressed about its credibility became well known. Our author places the responsibility for it on the Romans and seems to anticipate the objections that did not fail to appear. John the Deacon (*PL*, LXXV, 105) is concerned with the theological implications of the miracle. First of all, he makes it quite clear that the English are responsible for it, and, while not denying the truth of the other miracles he had heard through that source, he finds this one difficult to believe, for

so great a teacher would never have presumed to pray for the soul of a pagan, seeing that in the fourth book of the *Dialogues* (see Moricca, p. 305) he himself taught that one must not pray for dead infidels and sinners condemned to everlasting fire. He might also have added a reference to Gregory's fuller and more emphatic statement on the same subject in his *Moralia* (XXXIV, 19: *PL*, LXXVI, 739). John then proceeds to twist the story slightly rather than scrap it altogether. It does not say that he "prayed" but that he "wept"; further, Trajan was not necessarily freed from hell but only from the pain of his eternal tortures. Later on, St. Thomas Aquinas referred to the story in his *Summa Theologica* (suppl. to part iii, Q71. A5), questioning its veracity. Dante refers to it twice (*Purgatorio*, X, 73-93; *Paradiso*, XX, 106-17). In his version, as in a number of later versions, Trajan comes to life long enough to declare his faith. The story may possibly have its origin in an incident told by Dio Cassius about Hadrian (cf. Dio Cassius, *Roman History*, trans. E. Cary, Loeb Library series [London, 1925], LXIX, p. 435). The story relates that once when a woman made a request to him as he passed by on a journey, he at first said to her, "I have no time," but afterwards when she cried out, "Cease then being emperor," he turned about and granted her request. The story received an English dress in a surviving medieval poem. In it Gregory becomes St. Erkenwald (Bishop of London from 675 to 693), while Trajan becomes a British judge. When St. Paul's Church in London was being rebuilt, a tomb was opened up containing an undecayed corpse of a British judge. Erkenwald revived him long enough to allow the judge the reveal his identity. Because he had always been just in his judgments, the Bishop's tears that fell on his face were allowed to constitute baptism, and the judge was able to announce that his soul had just been received into Paradise. Immediately afterwards the body fell to dust. For a study of the extremely wide ramifications of the Trajan story all over Western Europe in the Middle Ages, see Gaston Paris, *La Légende de Trajan*, Bibliothèque de l'École des Hautes Études, Fasc. 35 (Paris, 1878), and also *Select Early English Poems,* ed. I. Gollancz, IV, "St Erkenwald" (London, 1922). This edition also contains a discussion of the Trajan story. It seems an extraordinary thing that two

of the best-known medieval legends, this and the story known as St. Gregory's Mass (see c. 20), should have originated from a remote monastery on the northeast coast of England.

[123] The third kind of baptism seems to be an invention of the author to avoid the difficulty of an unbaptized person getting into Paradise. The two other kinds of baptism were presumably baptism by water and baptism by blood, to cover the case of unbaptized people who suffered martyrdom for the faith, like the soldier who was executed for refusing to kill St. Alban and was "cleansed by the washing of his own blood" (*HE*, I, 8). Is there a possible reminiscence here of some ancient northern story, told many years later in the Prose Edda of Snorri Sturluson, of how Baldr died and was to be released from Hel if all creatures and created things would shed tears for him? *Prose Edda of Snorri Sturluson*, trans. J. I. Young (Cambridge, 1954), pp. 83-84.

[124] Trajan was Emperor from 98 to 117. He built the Forum Trajanum with its basilicas and libraries and a circular marble column in the centre 95 feet high, covered with a series of reliefs ascending spirally and commemorating his victories in his Dacian campaigns. Though we are not told what called the incident to mind, the words would suggest that whoever first told the tale saw it pictorially displayed somewhere in the Forum. It may have been on the Arch of Trajan, or perhaps he interpreted one of the reliefs in this way. It is not easy to see which of these could have been thus interpreted. But in any case it is most improbable that our author had any clear knowledge of what the Forum looked like. He does not even mention the column.

[125] The recompense would presumably be the blood-money. For an Englishman of the seventh century this was of supreme importance. If a man was killed it was the duty of his kindred to take vengeance on the slayer or to exact compensation. The woman was a widow and presumably had no close kinsfolk to exact compensation or take vengeance, and so she appealed to the Emperor. Doubtless our writer was interpreting the story in the light of the conditions he knew. Bede in his account of Edwin and Oswald emphasizes their care for the common people.

[126] Isaiah 1:17-18.

¹²⁷ See Cant. 8:6; Matth. 3:10; II Cor. 5:14. This expression of unworthiness and these excuses are slightly reminiscent of the regular patter of the prologue to the typical saint's Life written on the Antonian model. See Introduction, p. 48, and p. 140n*1*.

¹²⁸ See Matth. 21:12 and John 2:14-16; also Matth. 18:12 and Luke 15:4. Gregory also calls attention to the difference in the accounts of the two Evangelists in his *Homilies on the Gospels*, II, 34: *PL*, LXXVI, 1247.

¹²⁹ Lack of information about their subject is one of the commonest complaints of writers of saints' Lives. One of the ways in which they got over the difficulty was to borrow from other sources stories that had nothing at all to do with their subject. One such example is the miracle of the relic-clothes related in c. 21. See p. 153 n*83*. Our author's ingenious defense of this method of providing a saint with a dossier was perhaps intended to satisfy the occasional doubts that must have been felt by his readers or hearers when they recognized the same miracle as having been reported of various saints. See H. Delehaye, *The Legends of the Saints,* trans. D. Attwater (London, 1962), especially c. 2.

¹³⁰ The argument used here by our writer for his own purposes is based on a section of the *Regula Pastoralis* (III, 10: *PL,* LXXVII, 65) in which Gregory is condemning the envious by pointing out that, as we are all parts of the body of Christ, every limb assists and is indispensable to every other limb. So the good fortune of one is shared by all; and what we see and admire in others we do not need to envy, because it is truly ours too, seeing that we all belong to the same body. See I Cor. 12:12-22 and Rom. 12:5.

¹³¹ The reference is to the *Homilies on the Gospel*, II, 34. See p. 156n*103*.

¹³² The Vulgate reading of the passage (Prov. 4:7) is "posside sapientiam et in omni possessione tua acquire prudentiam." The writer is using an Old Latin version to which he would have access in Whitby; in fact he may have been using Jerome's Letter 52 to Nepotianus where Jerome quotes the passage not in his own (Vulgate) version but in this form, as in the text (*PL,* XXII, 528). See also Gen. 1:27; Matth. 18:11; John 15:9; John 14:12; Matth 13:49; Matth. 19:29; Rom. 5:8; Psa. 118 (119):104 and 99-100.

133 *Dial.* II, 16: Moricca, p. 104, and 1 Cor. 6:17. See also Rom. 5:5 and I Tim. 1:5.

134 The whole chapter is based on Gregory's *Regula Pastoralis*, I, 9: *PL,* LXXVII, 22, and III, Prol.: *PL,* LXXVII, 49. The book was dedicated to John, Bishop of Ravenna, who had gently reprimanded him for having shirked his duty as a leader of the church. Gregory seeks to show in this book how heavy are the duties of an ecclesiastical ruler. John was Bishop of Ravenna from 578 to 595 and a close friend of the saint until later on Gregory had to rebuke him for using the pallium at other times than at mass and generally for his presumption and duplicity. *MGH Epp.,* I, 295.

135 The third and longest book of the *Regula* is entirely devoted to the question of how a preacher should try to adapt his sermons to the various types of congregation he is likely to meet.

136 *Dial.,* Pref.: Moricca, p. 14.

137 Phil. 1:23; Psa. 54 (55):5 and Psa. 115 (116):15.

138 The writer seems to be echoing the famous phrase from the *Commonitorium* of St. Vincent of Lérins: *"quod semper, quod ubique, quod ad omnibus creditum est."* PL, L, 640.

139 The Council of *Cloveshoe* (the modern equivalent of the place is unidentified) in 747 gave instructions for his feast to be celebrated on 12 March. See Introduction, p. 19. His name was also placed in the canon of the mass in the Gallo-Roman rite.

140 See Luke 12:42; John 12:24-25; I John 3:24; Matth. 24:46-47; Psa. 115 (116):15.

141 The author has borrowed the details of the date of his death, the length of his episcopate, and the place of his burial from the *Liber Pontificalis* (ed. Mommsen, pp. 161-62). Bede also borrows these facts from the same source (*HE,* II, 1).

142 *Secretarium* is used in Medieval Latin both of the room in which bishops conducted their business and of the sacristy. The addition of the words *"eius officii"* seems to imply that our author is using the word in its former meaning. Ordinarily Bede seems to use the word in the sense of a sanctuary.

Select Bibliography
(See also books listed under "Abbreviations.")

Anderson, A. O., and Anderson, M. O., ed. *Adomnan's Life of Columba* (London, 1961).

Battiscombe, C. F., ed., *The Relics of St. Cuthbert* (Durham, 1956).

Blair, P. Hunter, *Introduction to Anglo-Saxon England* (Cambridge, 1956).

Brown, G. Baldwin, *The Arts in Early England*, 6 vols. (London, 1903-37).

[Bruce-Mitford, R. L. S.], *The Sutton Hoo Ship-Burial*, 2nd impression (British Museum, London, 1951).

Chadwick, N. K., ed., *Celt and Saxon: Studies in the Early British Border* (Cambridge, 1963).

ed., *Studies in the Early British Church* (Cambridge, 1958).

Poetry and Letters in Early Christian Gaul (London, 1955).

Charlesworth, M. P., ed., *The Heritage of Early Britain* (London, 1952).

Clemoes, P., ed., *The Anglo-Saxons: Studies Presented to Bruce Dickins* (London, 1959).

Colgrave, B., ed., *Felix's Life of St. Guthlac* (Cambridge, 1956).

The Earliest Saints' Lives Written in England, Sir Israel Gollancz Memorial Lecture, *Proceedings of the British Academy*, XLIV (1959), 35-60.

Colgrave, B., and Mynors, R. A. B., edd., *Bede's Ecclesiastical History of the English People* (Oxford, 1967).

Delehaye, H., *The Legends of the Saints*, trans. D. Attwater (London, 1962).

Duckett, E. S., *Alcuin, Friend of Charlemagne* (New York, 1951).

Anglo-Saxon Saints and Scholars (New York, 1947).

The Gateway to the Middle Ages (New York, 1938).

Dümmler, E., ed., *Epistolae Alcuini, MGH. Epp. IV* (Berlin, 1895).

Ehwald, R., ed., *Aldhelmi Opera, MGH. Auct. Ant. XV* (Berlin, 1919).

Select Bibliography

Gollancz, I., ed., *Select Early English Poems, IV*, "St. Erkenwald" (London, 1922).

Gougaud, L., *Christianity in Celtic Lands* (London, 1932).

Gregory the Great, *Dialogues*, ed. Moricca, U., *Fonti per la storia d'Italia* (Rome, 1924).
   Epistle to Leander and Moralia. PL, LXXV, 510-76, 782.
   Homilies on Ezekiel. PL, LXXVI, 785-1072.
   Homilies on the Gospels. PL, LXXVI, 1075-1312.
   Letters, ed. Ewald, P., and Hartmann, L., *MGH Epp.*, I, II,
   Regula Pastoralis. PL, LXVII, 13-128.

Haddan, A. W., and Stubbs, W., *Councils and Ecclesiastical Documents Relating to Great Britain and Ireland*, III (Oxford, 1878).

Jones, C. W., *Saints' Lives and Chronicles* (Ithaca, N.Y., 1947).

Kenney, J. F., *The Sources for the Early History of Ireland I, Ecclesiastical* (New York, 1929).

Laistner, M. L. W., *Thought and Letters in Western Europe A.D. 500-900* (London, 1957).

Levison, W., *England and the Continent in the Eighth Century* (Oxford, 1946).

Lowe, E. A., *Codices Latini Antiquiores, a Palaeographical Guide to Latin Manuscripts Prior to the Ninth Century*, 11 vols. (Oxford, 1934-66).

Meyvaert, P., *Bede and Gregory the Great: Jarrow Lecture 1964* (Jarrow, 1964).

Ogilvy, J. D. A., *Books Known to Anglo-Latin Writers from Aldhelm to Alcuin* (Cambridge, Mass., 1936).

Powicke, F. M., and Fryde, E. B., *Handbook of British Chronology* (London, 1961).

Quentin, H., *Les Martyrologes historiques du Moyen Âge* (Paris, 1908).

Ryan, J., *Irish Monasticism* (London, 1931).

Sisam, K., *Studies in the History of Old English Literature* (Oxford, 1953).

Whitelock, D., *The Beginnings of English Society, Penguin History of England II* (London, 1952).

Wright, C. E., *The Cultivation of Saga in Anglo-Saxon England* (Edinburgh, 1939).

Appendix

A list of passages quoted or referred to in the Introduction and in the Whitby *Life of St. Gregory* (numbers in parentheses are page references in this volume)

Adamnan
  Vita Columbae
    I, 21 (158n*117*)
    III, 6 (151n*74*)
Ælfflæd
  Letter to Adolana
    Tangl, No. 8 (40n*23*)
Æthelbald
  Charter
    (15n*5*)
Alcuin
  Epistles
    81 (50n*1*)
    116 (29n*27*)
    124 (19n*4*)
  Verses on the Saints of the Church of York
    388 ff. (43n*34*)
  Life of Willibrord
    c. 9 (145n*43*)
Aldhelm
  De laude virginitatis
    c. 55 (19n*4*)
  Letter to Gerontius
    (154n*92*)
Alfred the Great
  Verse preface to his translation of Gregory's *Regula Pastoralis*
    (28n*18*)
Athanasius
  Life of St. Antony
    (28, 140n*1*, 164n*127*)
Augustine
  De civitate Dei
    Book XV (156n*105*)

  De Trinitate
    Book III, 10, 21 (156n*105*)
Bede
  Ecclesiastical History
    I, 8 (163n*123*)
    I, 15 (144n*42*)
    I, 23 (3n*4*, 143n*22*)
    I, 27 (26n*14*, 149n*59*)
    I, 29 (146n*50*)
    I, 30 (27n*15*)
    I, 31 (27n*17*, 142n*14*)
    I, 32 (145n*42*)
    I, 1 (19n*3*, 56n*1*, 141n*8*, 144n*41*, 165n*141*)
    II, 3 (19n*1*, 147n*50*)
    II, 4 (147n*50*)
    II, 5 (4n*7*, 28n*19*, 147n*51*, 149n*59*)
    II, 6 (151n*74*)
    II, 9 (47n*3*)
    II, 12 (50n*2*, 149n*63*)
    II, 13 (151n*71*)
    II, 14 (5n*8*)
    II, 16 (5n*9*, 148n*52*, 150n*68*)
    II, 20 (19n*1*, 42n*31*, 53n*6*)
    III, 5 (145n*43*)
    III, 11 (43n*32*)
    III, 12 (6n*10*)
    III, 14 (36n*10*)
    III, 15 (53n*7*)
    III, 17 (7n*11*)
    III, 19 (16n*32*, 59n*5*)
    III, 24 (7n*12*, 42n*30*)
    III, 25 (9n*14*, 34n*5*)
    IV, 10 (59n*5*)

Appendix

IV, 12 (14n25)
IV, 19 (16n31, 158n117)
IV, 23 (5n8, 31n1, 33n3, 36 n12, 37n14)
IV, 24 (38n16)
IV, 25 (35n8)
IV, 26 (13n23, 48n5)
V, 2 (158n117)
V, 3 (37n15, 39n21)
V, 6 (158n117)
V, 23 (15n30, 18n38)
V, 24 (47n4, 142n19)

Homelia
I, 13 (11-12n19)
II, 5 (Opp. V, 5) (142n19)

Letter to Egbert
(29n26, 39n19)

Lives of the Abbots
cc. 4, 7 (11n18)
c. 11 (39n20)
c. 15 (12n20)
c. 17 (12n21)

Prose Life of St. Cuthbert
Prologue (59n6)
c. 23 (41n24, 41-42n29)
c. 24 (12n22, 41n25)

Bible
  Genesis
    1:27 (133, 164n132)
    1:28 (99, 149n62)
    28:12, 17, 19 (87, 144n35)
  I Samuel
    16:7 (83, 143n26)
  Job
    38:3 (123, 158n115)
  Psalms
    6:9 (85, 143n29)
    17 (18):12 (87, 144n35)
    18 (19):9 (91, 144n39)
    39 (40):4 (97, 149n61)
    44 (45):3 (119, 155n100)
    45 (46):5-7 (115, 117, 154 n95)
    54 (55):5 (137, 165n137)
    67 (68):36 (77, 142n12; 111, 153n85)
    77 (78):7 (73, 140n2)
    87 (88):6 (125, 159n119)
    88 (89):6 (95, 148n54)
    115 (116):15 (137, 165 n137; 139, 165n140)
    118 (119):99-100, 104 (135, 164n132)
  Proverbs
    4:7 (135, 164n132)
    14:33 (119, 155n100)
    21:20 (119, 155n100)
  Canticles
    8:6 (129, 164n127)
  Ecclesiasticus
    34:7 (103, 151n73)
  Isaiah
    1:17-18 (129, 163n126)
  Ezekiel
    1:25 (121, 156n107)
  Malachi
    2:6 (89, 91, 144n39)
  Matthew
    3:10 (129, 164n127)
    3:16 (121, 157n109)
    5:8 (121, 156n106)
    5:14, 16 (119, 156n102)
    5:15 (87, 144n35)
    6:20 (121, 156n106)
    11:11 (79, 142n17)
    11:28 (95, 97, 148n55)
    11:29 (85, 143n30)
    12:29 (83, 143n23)
    13:49 (133, 164n132)
    13:52 (121, 156n106)
    14:29 (85, 143n29)
    16:4 (81, 142n18)
    16:17 (107, 153n80)
    16:18 (125, 159n119)
    17:9 (123, 157n111)
    18:1 (85, 143n32)
    18:11 (133, 164n132)
    18:12 (131, 164n128)
    19:28 (133, 164n132)

21:12 (131, 164n*128*)
24:46-47 (139, 165n*140*)
25:33 (158n*112*)
26:39 (89, 144n*37*)
28:19 (97, 148n*57*)

Mark
16:14-20 (143n*28*)
16:15 (117, 155n*98*)

Luke
2:37 (87, 144n*34*)
8:15 (81, 143n*21*)
12:8 (119, 156n*102*)
12:42 (139, 165n*140*)
15:4 (131, 164n*128*)
15:8-9 (156n*103*)
21:19 (85, 143n*30*)

John
2:14-16 (131, 164n*128*)
6:15 (89, 144n*37*)
6:54 (107, 153n*81*)
6:57 (109, 153n*82*)
7:38 (119, 156n*104*)
12:24-25 (139, 165n*140*)
12:36 (89, 144n*37*)
14:6 (79, 142n*15*)
14:12 (79, 142n*16*; 133, 164 n*132*)
15:9 (133, 164n*132*)

Acts
9:41 (85, 143n*30*)
10:34, 35 (111, 153n*86*)
13:11 (85, 143n*29*)
15:9 (111, 153n*84*)

Romans
5:5 (135, 165n*133*)
5:8 (135, 164n*132*)
8:17 (81, 142n*20*)
9:22 (93, 145-46n*46*)
9:23 (97, 148n*57*)
12:5 (131, 164n*130*)
14:23 (111, 153n*84*)

I Corinthians
1:22 (81, 142n*18*)
2:7 (117, 155n*98*)
5:3 (83, 143n*23*)
6:17 (135, 165n*133*)
12:8-9 (83, 143n*25*)
12:11 (83, 143n*23*)
12:12-22 (131, 133, 164 n*130*)
13:1-3 (89, 91, 144n*39*)
14:22 (81, 142n*18*)

II Corinthians
5:14 (129, 164n*127*)
6:7-8 (123, 157-58n*112*)

Galatians
1:16 (113, 154n*88*)

Ephesians
2:10 (83, 143n*25*)
4:7 (83, 143n*25*)
5:2 (81, 143n*21*)
5:8 (83, 143n*23*)
6:13 (113, 154n*90*)

Philippians
1:23 (137, 165n*137*)
2:7-8 (89, 144n*38*)
2:8 (89, 144n*37*)

Colossians
1:15 (83, 143n*25*)
2:3 (83, 143n*27*)
2:12 (115, 154n*91*)

I Thessalonians
1:10 (101, 150n*66*)

James
1:17 (83, 143n*25*)

I Timothy
1:5 (135, 165n*133*)

Hebrews
7:10 (97, 148n*57*)
9:11-12 (89, 144n*37*)

I John
3:24 (139, 165n*140*)
4:17 (91, 144n*39*)

Revelation
19:6 (95, 148n*53*)

Boniface
Letters
73 (14n*28*, 18n*37*)

Appendix

Cicero
  De divinatione
    I, 39, 85 (149n60)
Dante
  Purgatorio
    X, 73-93 (162n122)
  Paradiso
    V, 600 (156n103)
    XX, 106-17 (162n122)
Dio Cassius
  Roman History
    LXIX (162n122)
Dionysius the Areopagite
  Concerning the Heavenly Hierarchies
    III, 119 ff. (156n103)
Eddius
  Life of Wilfrid
    c. 3 (9n13)
    c. 10 (9n14)
    c. 13 (154n89)
    c. 14 (9n15)
    c. 34 (10n16)
    c. 54 (36n11)
    c. 60 (41n28)
    c. 64 (14n28)
Eusebius
  Historia Ecclesiastica
    V, 28 (151n74)
Gregory
  Dialogues
    Preface (73, 141n6; 117, 154-55n96; 137, 165 n136)
    I, 2 (85, 143n31)
    I, 12 (79, 142n14)
    II, 11 (144n40)
    II, 16 (135, 165n133)
    II, 34 (150n68)
    III, 17 (83, 143n24)
    IV, 11 (150n68)
    IV, 40 (153n87)
    IV, 57 (158n118)
  Epistles
    IV, 30 (153n83)
    V, 15 (165n134)
    VI, 10 (145n43)
    VII, 29 (20n7)
    VIII, 29 (26n13)
    IX, 228 (25n12)
    X, 21 (20n7)
    XI, 20 (158n116)
    XI, 36 (142n14)
    XI, 55 (20n7)
  Homilies on Ezekiel
    I, 8 (121, 156n107)
    II, Pref. (154n94)
    II, 2 (141n10)
    II, 6 (30n28)
    II, 9 (123, 158n113)
    II, 10 (154n94)
  Homilies on the Gospels
    I, 4 (142n14)
    I, 10 (142n14)
    I, 12 (153n87)
    II, 27 (89, 144n38)
    II, 29 (79, 142n14; 85, 143 n28; 142n18; 143n24)
    II, 34 (156n103, 164n128)
  Moralia
    Epistle to Leander (75, 141 n8; 75, 77, 141n10; 123, 125, 158n116)
    II, 21 (151-52n76)
    XXVII, 11 (145n43)
    XXVII, 12 (142n18)
    XXXIV, 19 (162n122)
  Regula Pastoralis
    I, 9 (135, 137, 165n134)
    III, Prol. (135, 137, 165 n134)
    III, 10 (133, 164n130)
  Libellus Responsionum. See Bede, *Historia Ecclesiastica, I,* 27
Jerome
  Letters
    22 (151n74)
    46 (119, 155-56n101)
    52 (164n132)

John the Deacon
   Life of St. Gregory
      Prefatio (59n*1*)
      II, 41-44 (58n*4*, 152n77)
      II, 43 (161-62n*122*)
      II, 45 (52n*5*)
      IV, 13 (154n94)
      IV, 69 (157n*110*, 161n*121*)
      IV, 70 (51n*3*)
      IV, 83 (19-20n*6*; 73, 141n*4*)
      IV, 84 (157n*110*)
   Liber Pontificalis (Mommsen's edition)
      p. 161 (93, 141n*4*, 146-47 n*50*)
      pp. 161-62 (139, 165n*141*)
      p. 163 (161n*121*)
      p. 225 (14n27)
Nennius
   Historia Brittonum
      c. 63 (148n58)
Paul the Deacon
   Life of St. Gregory
      c. 13 (144n33)
      c. 19 (146n47)
      cc. 23-29 (152n77)
      c. 28 (157n*110*)
Prosper
   Continuation of Jerome's Chronicle
      (154n94)

Sulpicius Severus
   Life of St. Martin
      c. 1 (141-42n*11*)
Symeon of Durham
   Historia Dunelmensis Ecclesiae
      III, 1 (17n36)
      III, 21 (45n*38*)
   Life of St. Oswald
      c. 9 (4n*6*)
Tacitus
   Germania
      c. 10 (149n*60*)
Thomas Aquinas
   Summa Theologica
      suppl. to part iii, Q71. A 5 (162n*122*)
Vincent of Lérins
   Commonitorium Primum
      c. 2 (165n*138*)
Virgil
   Eclogues
      IX, 15 (149n*60*)
Vita Anonyma Cuthberti
      III, 6 (41n25)
      IV, 10 (41n26)
      IV, 17 (158n*117*)
William of Malmesbury
   Gesta Regum
      I, 56 (44n*37*)

Index

Acha, daughter of King Ælle, 2
Adamnan, a monk of Coldingham, 35
Adamnan of Iona, 151n74. *See also* Appendix
Administration, words of, 61, 107, 152n78
Adolana, Abbess of Pfalzel, 40
Æbbe, Abbess of Coldingham, 10
Æfflæd, daughter of King Oswiu, 8; entrusted to St. Hild, 8, 34; abbess of Whitby, 39, 42, 47, 103; Latin style of, 40; friend of Cuthbert, 40, 156n103; friend of Wilfrid, 41; translates Edwin's relics, 42, 43; date of death of, 48. *See also* Appendix
Ælfwald, King of East Anglia, 15
Ælfwig, a monk of Evesham, 45
Ælle (Ælli), King of Deira, 1, 2, 3, 31, 46, 91, 95, 97
Æthelbald, King of Mercia, 15; *rex Anglorum*, 15; murdered, 15. *See also* Appendix
Æthelberht, Archbishop of York, 18
Æthelberht, King of Kent, 4, 16, 26-27, 95; *rex Anglorum*, 145n42; *Bretwalda*, 147n51; code of laws of, 147n51
Æthelburh, daughter of King Æthelberht, 4, 5
Æthelburh, daughter of King Anna, 16
Æthelfrith, King of Northumbria, 2, 3, 32
Æthelhere, King of East Anglia, 7
Æthelred, King of Mercia, 14; attacks Kent, 14; retires to Bardney, 14, 47; wins back Lindsey, 42-43
Æthelthryth, St. (St. Etheldreda or St. Audrey), daughter of King Anna: marries King Ecgfrith, 10; becomes a nun, 10; establishes monastery at Ely, 16; translation of her incorrupt body, 16, 43
Æthelwald, King of East Anglia, 15
Ætla, Bishop of Dorchester, 37
Agilulf, King of Lombards, 154n94
Agnofleda, St., 66
Aidan, St.: helps to reconvert Northumbria, 6; friend of Oswine, 6; death of, 7; meets St. Hild, 32; buried on right of altar, 158n112
Alban, St., 58, 163n123
Alcuin, 18, 19, 29, 50. *See also* Appendix
Aldfrith, King of Northumbria: half Irish, 13; patron of the arts, 13; expels Wilfrid, 13; peaceful reign of, 13; death of, 17; accession prophesied by Cuthbert, 41; stepbrother of Ælfflæd, 41
Aldhelm, 19. *See also* Appendix
Aldwulf, King of East Anglia, 15, 32
Alfred the Great. *See* Appendix
Alhfrith, sub-king of Deira, son of Oswiu: friend of Wilfrid, 9, 36; encourages Council of Whitby, 9, 40; wishes to go to Rome, 9
Ambrose, St., 37, 143n33, 156n101
Ammonius, a monk of Nitria, 144n33
Andrew, St., monastery of, 20, 145 n45, 157n110
Angels, 91, 119, 123, 133; hierarchies of, 156n103
Angli: use of term, 144-45n42
Anglia, East. *See* East Anglia
Anguli, 91, 144-45n42
Anna, King of East Anglia, 10, 15, 32
"Apocrisarius," title given to Gregory by Pope, 22
Archdeacon, 40, 109
Arian heresy, 25
Arx, Ildefons von, 65
Athanasius, St., 37, 143n33. *See also* Appendix
Attila, King of the Huns, 154n94
Augustine, St., of Canterbury: fears for journey, 3; received by Æthelberht, 3, 16; success of his mission, 3; receives pallium, 26; sends questions to and receives answers from Gregory, 26-27, 148-49n59
Augustine, St., of Hippo, 37, 54, 143 n33, 156n101. *See also* Appendix

Baldr, 163n123
Bamborough, 6
Baptism, 26, 35, 151-52n76; by tears, 52, 162n122; by blood, 163n123
Bardney, 14, 35, 42, 44, 151n71

174

Barking, 35, 58
Bede, the Venerable, 3, 18; familiar with Gregory's works, 28, 156 n*101;* his visions of the afterlife, 29; recommends *Regula Pastoralis,* 29; his attitude to miracles, 58; uses Gregory's epistles, 53; his knowledge of classical authors, 54; his Latin style, 55; his relation to the Whitby *Life,* 56-59; his use of earlier Lives, 59; loses touch with Whitby, 59; variations from the Whitby *Life* in his work, 144n*41,* 147n*51,* 149n*63;* his use of word *secretarium,* 165n*142*
—*Ecclesiastical History,* 18, 24, 26, 53, 145n*43,* 155n99, 163n*123;* Letter to Egbert, 39; *Martyrology,* 49; *Prose Life of St. Cuthbert,* 41, 59. See also Appendix
Belisarius, 20
Benedict, St., of Nursia, 29, 144n*40,* 150n*68*
Benedict I, Pope, 21, 56, 91, 93, 145 n*45*
Benedictine Rule, 9
Beowulf, 148n*52*
Bernicia, 1, 5, 6, 13, 32, 35
Bertha, wife of Æthelberht, King of Kent, 3, 26, 147n*51*
Beverstone, Gloucester, 152n*77*
Bible, the, 12; Vulgate Version, 54, 66, 164n*132;* Old Latin versions, 54, 164n*132.* See also Appendix
Biblical exegesis, 22-23, 36, 148n*57*
Biscop, Benedict (Baducing): his first journey to Rome, 8, 40; second journey, 10; third journey, 10; fourth journey, 11; establishes Wearmouth monastery, 11; fifth journey, 11; sixth journey, 11; cautions monks about appointment of abbot, 39
Blood-money, 163n*125*
Boniface, Archdeacon, 40
Boniface, St., 14, 18, 29. See also Appendix
Bosa, Bishop of York, 37
Bosel, Bishop of the Hwicce (Worcester), 37
Bradwell-on-Sea, 16
Bregoswith, mother of St. Hild, 31
Bretwaldan, 4, 147n*51,* 147n*52*
British Church. See Celtic Church
British judge, 162n*122*
British pilgrims, 2

Index

Britons, 2, 6, 38; conquered by Saxons, 6; refuse to evangelize Saxons, 6
Bruide mac Beli, King of Picts, 13
Brunhild, Queen of Austrasia, 25
Burgh Castle, 16

Cadfan, King of North Wales, 4
Cædmon, 38
Cædwalla (Cadwallon), King of Gwynedd, 5
Caelian Hill, 20, 21, 141n*4*
Candidus, a priest, 145n*43*
Canisius, 60
Canonization, 140n*3*
Canterbury, 147n*51;* altar to Gregory, 19, 44, 105; see at, 26; school at, 27, 37; traditions, 53, 141n*4,* 143 n22
Canterbury Gospels. See Manuscripts
Catalogue of St. Gall MSS, 64
Cedd, Bishop of Essex, 16, 158n*112*
Celtic Church: difference from Roman Church, 2, 35; suspect to Saxons, 6
Celtic peoples, 2
Cenred, King of Mercia, 14; dies in Rome, 14
Cenred, King of Northumbria, 18
Centwine, King of Wessex, 10
Ceolfrith, first abbot of Jarrow, 11
Ceolred, King of Mercia, 14; condemned by St. Boniface, 14, 17-18
Ceolwulf, King of Northumbria: *HE* dedicated to him by Bede, 18; forcibly tonsured, 18; enters Lindisfarne, 18
Ceorl, 103, 105, 151n*72*
Cerdic (Ceretic), King of Elmet, 31
Chad (Ceadda), Bishop of York and Lichfield: replaces Wilfrid, 10; founds monastery at Lastingham, 16; his body at Lichfield, 43; does not wish to become bishop, 143n*33*
Charibert, King of Paris, 3, 147n*51*
Chelles, 32, 33
Childebert II, King of Austrasia, 25
Chlotar II, King of Neustria, 25
Chrysostom, John, 155n99
Chur, 66
Church, the, Christ's body, 131, 164 n*130*
Churches: St. Andrew's, Hexham, 9; St. Augustine's, Canterbury, 19; St. Gregory's, Kirkdale, 41; St. John Lateran, Rome, 59; St. Martin's, Canterbury, 3; St. Martin's, Tours,

Index

66; St. Paul's, Jarrow, 11; St. Peter's, Bradwell-on-Sea, 16; St. Peter's, Hackness, 39; St. Peter's Peterborough, 151n*75;* St. Peter's, Ripon, 9, 151n*75;* St. Peter's, Rome, 139, 161n*121;* St. Peter's, Selsey, 151n*75;* St. Peter's, Wearmouth, 11, 151n*75;* St. Peter's, Whitby, 105; St. Peter's, York, 9, 19, 42, 151n*75;* S. Maria Maggiore, Rome, 24

Ciacconius (Alfonso Chacon), 157 n*110*

Cicero. See Appendix

Cloveshoe, Synod of, 19, 165n*139*

Coins, story of three, 125, 159n*118*

Coldingham, monastery of, 10, 34, 35

Colman, Bishop of Lindisfarne, 9

Columba, St., 151n*74*

Constantina, wife of Emperor Mauricius Tiberius, 153n*83*

Constantinople, 21-23

Coquet Island, 41

Corporal, Gregory's use of a, 153n*79*

Crisaurius, 153n*87*

Crow, as an omen, 51, 97, 99, 149n*60*

Cuthbert, St.: prior and bishop of Lindisfarne, 12; bishop of Hexham, 12; hermit, 12; visits Carlisle, 12; dies, 13; buried at Lindisfarne on right of altar, 13, 157n*111;* elevation of his relics, 17; growth of his cult, 17, 43, 141n*3;* his incorrupt body, 17; friend of Ælfflæd, 40; prophesies death of Ecgfrith and accession of Aldfrith, 41; Life by Bede, 41, 49; Life by Lindisfarne monk, 49, 59; does not wish to become bishop, 143n*33*

Cwenburh, a nun at Watton, 39

Danish Boys, 145n*43*

Dante, 29, 156n*103*, 162n*122*. See also Appendix

David, psalmist, 135

Deira, 1, 5, 8, 13, 31, 35, 46, 91, 145 n*44*

Devils, 113

Dio Cassius, 162n*122*. See also Appendix

Dionysius the Areopagite, 156n*103*. See also Appendix

Dove: dictates to Gregory, 51, 58; departure of soul in form of, 150n*68*

Dreams, 31, 38, 47, 103, 105, 151n*74*

Dunstan, St., 143n*33*

Durham Cathedral, 17

Eadberht, Bishop of Lindisfarne, 17

Eadberht, King of Northumbria, 18

Eadfrith, Bishop of Lindisfarne, 17

Ealdwine, a monk of Winchcomb, 45

Eanbald, King of Kent, 149n*59*

Eanbald II, Archbishop of York, 29

Eanflæd, daughter of Edwin, King of Northumbria: marries Oswiu, 7, 39, 53; taken to Kent, 7, 53; protector of Wilfrid, 8, 40; goes to Whitby after Oswiu's death, 36; baptized by Paulinus, 39, 53; abbess of Whitby, 42, 103; helps in translation of Edwin's relics, 42, 43, 44; date of death, 47; Welsh story of her baptism, 148n*58*

East Anglia, 3, 7, 10, 15, 32, 99

Easter dates and tables, 2, 35, 39

Eata, Abbot of Melrose, 12

Eata, father of King Eadberht, 18

Ecgfrith, King of Northumbria: hostage of Penda, 8; marries Æthelthryth, 10; nephew of Æbbe, 10; marries Iurminburg, 10; expels Wilfrid, 10; gives land to Benedict Biscop, 11; killed at Nechtansmere, 12-13, 42, 156n*103;* his death prophesied, 41

Ecgric, King of East Anglia, 15

Edda, Prose, 163n*123*

Eddius, biographer of Wilfrid, 41, 59, 148n*52*, 154n*89*. See also Appendix

Edwin, King of Northumbria: at Rædwald's court, 3, 4, 31, 99; exiled in North Wales, 4, 31; put on throne of Northumbria, 4, 15, 32; baptized at York, 5, 31, 95, 97; killed at battle of Hatfield Chase, 5, 32, 39; overthrows Æthelfrith at River Idle, 15, 32, 149n*64;* annexes Elmet, 32; his relics translated to Whitby, 42, 46-47, 51, 103, 105; his head at York, 42; date of translation, 47; grandfather of Ælfflæd, 47, 103; father of Eanflæd, 47, 103; Paulinus appears to, 48, 50, 99, 101; Welsh story of baptism of, 148 n*58;* destroys heathen temples, 151 n*71;* his care for common people, 163n*125*

Egbert, Archbishop of York, 18, 39

Elmet, a British kingdom, 31, 32

Ely, 16, 35, 43

Eorcenberht, King of Kent, 9, 16

Eorpwald, son of King Rædwald, 15

Erkenwald, St., 162n*122*

Essex, 16, 26

Eulogius, Patriarch of Alexandria, 26
Eusebius. *See* Appendix
Eutychius, Patriarch of Constantinople, 23
Evesham, 45
Ezekiel, 123

Faremoûtiers-en-Brie, 16
Farne Island, 12, 41
Felix, biographer of St. Guthlac, 29
Finger, little, 107
Firmament, 121, 156n*108*
Foretelling by augury, 97, 149n*60*
Frankish kingdom, 2, 18, 25, 145n*43*
Fursa, an Irish monk, 16, 58
Fylgja, 150n*68*

Gall, St., Switzerland, viii, 60, 61, 63, 64, 66
Gaul, 2, 10, 16
Gaulish workmen, 11
Gilling, 40
Glass, 11
Goar, St., 64, 65
Golden Legend, The, 152n*77*
Gordianus, father of Gregory, 19, 73
Gospels, illuminated, 17, 44
Goths, 20
Gregory the Great, St.: his views on future of Europe, 1, 24; meets English youths, 1, 21, 46, 56, 91, 144 n*41*, 147n*51*; starts out for England, 1, 28, 56, 57, 93; sends missionaries to England, 3, 25-26; encourages St. Augustine, 3; altars dedicated to, 19, 44, 105; cult of, 19, 44, 46, 59, 73, 77, 81, 140n*3*; feast day of, 19, 165n*139*; birth, 19, 73; his mother's name, Sylvia, 19, 54, 58, 73, 141n*4*; education of, 20; knew no Greek, 20; appointed Prefect, 20; appointed Seventh Deacon, 21; his seven years in Constantinople, 22-23, 75; disputes with Eutychius, 23; attempts to avoid papacy, 23, 87, 143n*33*; appointed Pope, 23-24, 85, 93; autobiographical writings of, 29, 141n*8*; ill-health of, 30, 123, 158n*116*; death of, 30, 137, 165n*141*; references to in *Liber Pontificalis,* 37, 165n*141*; traditions about, 51; and the white dove that dictates *Homilies on Ezekiel,* 51, 58, 123, 157 n*110*; portraits of, 51, 157n*110*; slays his successor, 51, 58, 127; miracles performed by, 52, 56, 79, 81, 105, 107, 109, 111, 113, 115, 117, 125, 129, 131; rescues Trajan from hell, 52, 58, 127, 129; Roman citizens' reaction to, 56, 93; and story of locust, 56, 57, 93; quells demon-possessed horse, 58, 113, 115; and the unbelieving matron, 58, 61, 105, 107, 109; and the relic rags, 58, 109, 111, 164n*129*; MS of his Life, 63-69; his views on the active and contemplative life, 75, 141n*10*; *papa apostolicus,* 79, 142 n*13*; apostle of the English, 19, 83, 143n*22*; his attitude to miracles, 83, 85, 142n*14*, 142n*18*; gift of prophecy of, 91, 144n*40*; Mass of, 107, 152n*77*, 163n*122*; prescribes diet for Agilulf, 117, 154-55n*96*; called 'golden-mouthed,' 117, 155n*99*; his views on orders of angels, 119, 121, 156n*103*; seen with dove by intimate friend, 123, 157n*110*, 157 n*111*; binds physician in hell, 125; apologizes for leaving pastoral duties, 135, 137, 165n*134*; place of burial of, 139, 165n*141*; his views on baptism, 151-52n*76*; puts out lights on Siricius's tomb, 125, 159-61n*120*; his library threatened by Romans, 157n*110*; his views on prayers for pagans, 161-62n*122*. *See also* Appendix
Gwynedd, 5, 14

Hackness, 38-39, 44, 45; cross in church at, 44
Hadrian, Abbot of Canterbury, 27
Hadrian, Emperor, 162n*122*
Hartlepool, 33, 34, 37; name slabs at, 33, 44
Hatfield (Chase), Battle of, 5, 53, 103, 151n*71*
Heiu, Abbess of Hartlepool, 33
Hereric, father of St. Hild, 31, 32
Hereswith, sister of St. Hild, 31, 32, 33
Hexham, 18; bisphoric of, 12; crypt in the cathedral at, 153n*83*
High places, 113, 154n*89*
Hilarius, St., 64, 65
Hild, St., great-niece of Edwin: baptized, 5, 31; abbess of Whitby, 5, 33; Ælfflæd put under her care, 8, 34; born in Elmet, 31; takes refuge in East Anglia, 32; meets Aidan, 32; takes the veil, 32; called back to Northumbria, 33; abbess of

Index

monastery near River Wear, 33; abbess of Hartlepool, 33; her pupils at Whitby, 33, 37, 155n*99;* accepts Roman discipline, 36; opposes Wilfrid, 36; five of her ex-pupils bishops, 37; her illness and death, 38, 59; her influence on Church, 38
Horace, 54
Horse, demon-possessed, quelled by Gregory, 58, 113, 115
Humber, river, 8, 147-48n*52*
Humbrians, 45, 95, 147-48n*52*
Hwicce, 33, 37

Ida, King of Bernicia, 2
Idle, battle of the River, 15, 32, 149 n*64*
Iona, 5, 158n*117*
Irish bishop, 9
Irish clergy, 16
Irish monasteries, 5, 33, 39
Irish monks, 6, 16
Irish people, 6
Irish pilgrims, 2
Isidore, St., 37
Iurminburg, wife of King Ecgfrith, 10

Jacob, 87, 123
Jarrow, 11, 18, 37, 38, 44, 55
Jerome, St., 54, 87, 119, 155-56n*101;* 164n*132;* visits Siricius, 125, 159-61n*120;* scourged, 151n*74;* lost Life of, at Whitby, 160n*120.* See also Appendix
Job, 123, 125
Job, Book of, 22
Johannes, companion of St. Augustine, 147n*50*
John, St., the Baptist, 79, 121
John, St., of Beverley, 13, 37, 39
John the Deacon: doubts Trajan story, 52, 161-62n*122;* had a copy of Whitby *Life,* 52, 56; his debts to the Whitby *Life,* 52, 56; knew name of Gregory's mother, 141n*4;* variant story of white dove, 157 n*110*
—*Life of St. Gregory,* 19-20, 59-60, 144n*33,* 152n*78,* 152n*79,* 153n*83,* 154n*89,* 154n*92,* 155n*99,* 161-62 n*122.* See also Appendix
John VIII, Pope, 59
John, Bishop of Ravenna, 135, 165 n*134*
Justin II, Emperor, 21
Justinian, Emperor, 20
Justus, a monk, 158n*118*

Kent, 2-3, 4, 9, 26, 39, 147n*51*
Kirkdale, 41

Lastingham, 16
Laurentius, Archbishop of Canterbury, 26, 93, 146-47n*50;* scourged, 151 n*74*
Leander, Bishop of Seville, 22, 25, 28, 29, 158n*116*
Leeds, 8
Left hand, 123, 157-58n*112*
Leo I, Pope, 153n*83*
Lérins, 2
Libellus Responsionum, 27, 57, 149 n*59.* See also Appendix
Liber Pontificalis, 14, 37, 54, 146n*50,* 159n*120,* 161n*121.* See also Appendix
Libraries, 12, 37
Lichfield, 43
Lindisfarne, 6, 8, 17, 18, 34, 37, 40, 50; bishopric of, 12; Lindisfarne Gospels, 17, 44; anonymous monk of, author of Life of St. Cuthbert, 36-37, 49; physicians at, 158n*117*
Lindisfarnenses, 150n*71*
Lindsey, 14, 103; held alternately by Northumbria and Mercia, 42, 150-51n*71;* finally recovered by Mercia, 42-43; inhabitants called *Lindisfari,* 150n*71*
Litanies, 139
Locust, story of the, 56, 57, 93, 146 n*48*
Lombards, 20, 23, 51, 59-60; their king healed, 58, 115, 117, 154n*94*
Lonochil, St., 64, 66
Lucius, St., 64, 65
Luz, 87

Magicians, story of the, 113, 115
Manuscript of St. Gall (part of Codex 567), 63-69; contents, 63-66; rebinding, 64; binding, 65; pagination, 65; palimpsest leaves, 65-66; origin, 66; handwriting, 67-68; corrector, 68-69
Manuscripts: from Rome, 12; Codex Amiatinus (Florence), 12; Lindisfarne Gospels (British Museum, London, Cotton Nero D. iv.), 17; Canterbury Gospels (Corpus Christi College, Cambridge [C.C.C.C. 286]), 27; Rule of St. Benedict (Oxford, Bodleian, Hatton 48 [3684]), 27-28
Marriages, illegal, 97, 148-49n*59*
Martin, St., 64, 66, 143n*33*

Matron, story of the unbelieving, 58, 61, 105, 107, 109
Matthew, St., 54, 131. *See also* Appendix
Maurice, Emperor, 23
Mellitus, Archbishop of Canterbury, 26, 27, 93, 146-47n50
Mercia: supreme in southern England, 23; controlling upper Thames, 37-38; relations with Lindsey, 42-43, 150-51n71
Miracles, 27, 29, 43, 58, 79, 81, 129, 131, 133; attributed wrongly to Gregory, 131, 133. *See also* Gregory

Narses, 20
Natalicia of saints, 81, 142n19
Natalius, 151n74
Nechtansmere, battle of, 12-13
Nennius. *See* Appendix
Nidd, river, 41
Norse legends, 154n89, 161n121
Northumbria, 1, 3, 4, 8, 16-17; devastated by Mercians and Britons, 5; declines in power, 13, 14, 17

Œthelwald, son of Oswald, 7
Offa, King of Mercia, 43, 155n99
Offa of Essex, 14
Oftfor, Bishop of the Hwicce, 33, 37, 155n99
Omens, 97, 99, 149n60
Osfrith, son of Edwin, 5
Osingadun, 41
Osred, King of Northumbria, 17
Osric, King of Northumbria, 18
Osthryth: wife of Æthelred, 14, 42; daughter of King Oswiu and of Eanflæd, 14, 42; translates Oswald's relics, 43
Ostrogoths, 25
Oswald, King of Northumbria: son of Æthelfrith, 5; educated at Iona, 5; unites Deira and Bernicia, 5-6; restores Christianity to Northumbria, 6; killed fighting against Penda, 6, 32; last words of, 6; relics translated to Bardney, 43; head in St. Cuthbert's coffin, 43; miracles of, 58; cult of, 141n3; *Bretwalda*, 147n51; his care for common people, 163n125
Oswine, King of Deira, 6-7, 40; killed by Oswiu, 7, 36
Oswiu, King of Northumbria: brother of Oswald, 5; educated at Iona, 5; rules Bernicia, 6; marries Eanflæd, 7; acquires Deira by killing Oswine, 7, 36; defeats and slays Penda, 8, 33; makes a vow, 8, 34; calls Council of Whitby, 9, 35; death of, 10, 39; his illegitimate son, King Aldfrith, 13; sends Cedd to Essex, 16; gives daughter Ælfflæd into Hild's care, 34, 39; *Bretwalda*, 147n51

Paignton, Devon, 152n77
Pallium, 26, 37
Paris, 3, 32, 147n51
Paul, St., the Apostle, 153n83
Paul the Deacon: Life of Gregory, 58, 59-60; 144n41, 152n77, 155n99; interpolated version of the Life, 58, 144n33, 146n47, 152n77, 152n78, 154n92, 161n121. *See also* Appendix
Paulinus, St., 6, 8, 46; brings Æthelburh to Northumbria, 4; flees from Northumbria, 5; appears to Edwin, 48, 50, 101; traditions concerning, 50-51; Bede's account of his appearance to Edwin, 50, 149n63; and story of the crow, 50-51, 97, 99, 150n68; death of, 46, 51; his soul carried to heaven in form of swan, 51, 57, 101, 150n68; as source of Gregory traditions, 53
Pelagius II, Pope, 21, 23, 146n49
Penda, King of Mercia: overthrows Edwin, 5, 43; overthrows Oswald, 6, 32, 43; attacks Oswiu, 7-8, 33; killed at battle of Winwæd, 8, 33; his swift rise to power, 15
Peter, St., the Apostle, 123; dedication of churches to, 151n75
Peter the Deacon, 29, 157n110, 157n111
Peter, a priest, 146n50
Pfalzel, near Treves, 40
Physicians, 115, 125, 154n92, 158n117
Picts, 13
Pilgrimages to shrines, 43, 140n3
Pippin, King of the Franks, 18
Plagues, 9, 16, 23
Plenitudo, 122, 123, 158n113
Powys, kingdom of North Wales, 14
Prologues, 140n1, 164n127
Prosper. *See* Appendix

Rædwald, King of East Anglia, 15, 50; overcomes Æthelfrith, 3; pro-

Index

tects Edwin, 3, 48, 99, 149n64; accepts Christianity, then relapses, 4
Rægenhere, son of Rædwald, 15
Ravenna, 135, 165n134
Reccared, King of Spain, 25
Reinfrid, a monk of Evesham, 45
Relics, 11, 43, 58, 105, 109, 111, 140 n3, 153n83
Repton, 35
Right hand, 123, 157-58n112
Ripon, 9; crypt in cathedral at, 153 n83
Rome, 1, 24, 51, 105, 113, 125, 127, 152n78, 153n83; bishop of, 2; journeys and pilgrimages to, 8-12, 14; troubles in, 20-21, 23, 30; St. John's Gate, 161n121; Pons Mulvia, 161 n121
Roman Church and discipline, 8, 10, 12, 35
Roman remains, 12, 16
Roman roads, 151n71
Romanus, priest to Eanflæd, 39, 53
Rum map Urbgen, a British priest, 148n58

Sabianus, Pope, 58, 125, 127; death of, 161n121
Saints: cult of, 140-41n3; scourging of, 151n74
Saxons conquer Britain, 6
Scholastica, St., 150n68
Seal: (or bull) of Boniface, 40; of Gregory, 109
Seckington, Staffordshire, 15
Secretarium, 138, 165n142
Secundinus, Bishop of Taormina, 155 n97
Sexburh, St., 16; becomes abbess of Ely, 16; translates the relics of Æthelthryth, 16
Sigeberht, King of East Anglia, 15
Sigeberht, King of Essex, 16
Silvester, St., 64, 65
Siricius, Pope, 125, 127, 159-61n120
Slapton, Northamptonshire, 152n77
Snorri Sturluson, Prose Edda of, 163 n123
Solomon, King, 135
South English, 103
Spain, 22, 25
Spirits, revenant, 105
Stoke Charity, Hampshire, 152n77
Streoneshealh: meaning of name, 34, 44. *See* Whitby
Sudranglorum. *See Sundaranglorum*
Suffragan bishops, 26

Sulpicius, St., 37, 48, 140n1. *See also* Appendix
Sundaranglorum, 102, 150n69
Sutton Hoo, 4, 15
Swan, 51, 57, 101, 150n68
Sylvia, mother of Gregory, 19, 54, 73, 141n4; portrait of, 141n4
Symeon of Durham, 45. *See also* Appendix

Tacitus, 149n60. *See also* Appendix
Tadcaster, 33
Tears, baptism by, 52, 127, 129, 162 n122
Theodore of Tarsus, Archbishop of Canterbury, 10, 37; his influence on the Church, 10; persuades Aldfrith to take Wilfrid back, 13; his school at Canterbury, 27, 37
Theoderic, King of Burgundy, 25
Theudebert, King of Austrasia, 25
Thomas Aquinas, St., 162n122. *See also* Appendix
Tiber, river, 23
Tiberius II, Emperor, 21, 22, 23
Tilbury, Essex, 16
Tonsure, 2, 35
Totila, King of the Goths, 20
Trajan, Emperor: rescued from hell by Gregory, 52, 58, 127, 129, 161-63n122; orthodoxy of story about, 52; his forum at Rome, 127, 163 n124; his kindness to a widow, 129; his column at Rome, 163 n124; his arch at Rome, 163n124
Transubstantiation, doctrine of, 61, 107, 109, 152n77
Trimma, priest of the South English, 47, 56, 103, 105
Tuda, Bishop, 9

Ultrahumbrenses, 148n52

Veritas, a title of Christ, 79, 142n15
Versions of the Bible. *See* Bible
Vestments, 107, 153n79
Vikings, 17
Vincent, St., of Lérins, 165n138. *See also* Appendix
Virgil, 13, 54. *See also* Appendix
Visigoths, 22, 25
Visions, 12, 29, 103
Vita Anonyma Cuthberti. *See* Appendix

Wall paintings, 152n77
Watton, Yorkshire, 39

Wærferth, Bishop of Worcester, 155 n99
Wear, river, 11, 33
Wearmouth, 11, 18, 37, 38, 45
Wenlock, Shropshire, 35
West Angles, 98, 99, 149n65
Whitby (*Streunes-alae, Streuneshealh*): Abbess Hild of, 5; Abbess Eanflæd of, 5, 35-36; Council at, 9, 12, 16, 35, 40; Gregory altar at, 19, 44, 105, 152n77; teaching and scholars at, 33, 36, 37; monastic site of buildings of, 34; double monastery of, 34-35; library at, 37; cell of, at Hackness, 38-39; Abbess Ælfflæd of, 39; cell of, at *Osingadun*, 41; Edwin's relics translated to, 42, 46, 51, 101, 103, 105; sculpture at, 44; excavations at, 44; destroyed by Danes, 44; rebuilt, 45; dissolved by Henry VIII, 45; date of translation of Edwin's relics to, 46-47; kings buried at, 105; road to Hatfield Chase from, 151n71; Jerome's works known at, 155-56 n101; possible lost Life of Jerome at, 160n120
Whitby *Life of St. Gregory*: date of, 45-49, 99, 103; its relationship with John the Deacon's Life, 46, 51, 56, 59-60; known on Continent, 53; its relationship with Bede, 56-59; editions of, 61-62; translations of, 63
Whitby Monk, author of the *Life*: his knowledge of Gregory's works, 28-29, 53; Latin style of, 36, 55-56; his knowledge of the Bible, 36, 53-54; his knowledge of other writers, 36-37, 54; facts ascertainable about, 45-46; two sections of his *Life*, 46, 52; complains of lack of information, 50-52, 129, 131, 133, 164 n129; his dependence on tradition, 50-53; as transition between sagamaker and writer, 52; did not know Gregory's Epistles, 53; his favorite parts of Bible, 54; apologizes for order of miracles, 131; aware of Edwin's supremacy, 148 n52; did not know *Libellus Responsionum*, 149n59
Wihtred, King of Kent, 149n59
Wilfrid, St.: travels with Benedict Biscop, 8; educated at Lindisfarne, 8; protege of Eanflæd, 8, 40; goes to Rome, 9; friend of Alhfrith, 9; at Council of Whitby, 9, 36; appointed bishop of Northumbria, 9; rules his see for only twenty of forty-six years of his episcopacy, 9; builds churches, 9, 153n83; introduces Benedictine Rule, 9; supplanted by Chad, 10; goes to Gaul, 10; restored by Theodore, 10; persuades Æthelthryth to take the veil, 10; quarrels with Ecgfrith, 10; appeals to Rome, 10; returns to Northumbria, 11; takes over diocese of Lindisfarne, 13; quarrels with Aldfrith, 13; opposed by Hild, 36; consecrates Oftfor, 37; friend of Ælfflæd, 41; buried at Ripon, 43; his Life by Eddius, 59; brings home relics, 153n83; wrecked on Sussex coast, 154n89; defeats magicians, 154n89
William the Conqueror, 45
William of Malmesbury, 44. *See also* Appendix
Willibrord, 145n43
Wimborne, Dorset, 35
Winchcomb, Gloucester, 45
Winwæd, river, 8, 33, 39
Witnesses of miracles, 157n111
Worcester, 155n99, 159-60n120
Wulfhere, King of Mercia, 8, 14
Wyverstone, Suffolk, 152n77

York, 5, 9, 31, 42; school at, 18; monastery at, 18; Gregory altar at, 19, 44; see at, 26, 37

Printed in the United Kingdom
by Lightning Source UK Ltd.
121045UK00001B/228